MW00935171

A COACH FOR ALL SEASONS

THE ROY MELVIN STORY

by
Stuart Melvin

Order this book online at www.trafford.com/06-2861
or email orders@trafford.com

Most Trafford titles are also available at major online book retailers.

Note for Librarians: A cataloguing record for this book is available from Library and Archives Canada at www.collectionscanada.ca/amicus/index-e.html

Printed in Victoria, BC, Canada.

ISBN: 978-1-4251-1102-1

www.trafford.com

North America & international
toll-free: 1 888 232 4444 (USA & Canada)
phone: 250 383 6864 ♦ fax: 250 383 6804 ♦ email: info@trafford.com

The United Kingdom & Europe
phone: +44 (0)1865 722 113 ♦ local rate: 0845 230 9601
facsimile: +44 (0)1865 722 868 ♦ email: info.uk@trafford.com

10 9 8 7 6 5 4 3 2

This book is dedicated to my brother Tom who died in 1997. During Dad's last years Tom was his primary caregiver. In this role he came to more deeply understand and appreciate the unusual man who was his father. Although Tom never participated in high school athletics, in every other way, he was his father's son.

ACKNOWLEDGMENTS

MANY PEOPLE and organizations contributed to the material in this book or helped jog my memory. Thanks to the Wisconsin Historical Society for the use of their microfilm of old newspapers, notably the *Ashland Daily Press, Iron County Miner, Ironwood Times/ Globe, Milwaukee Sentinel, Superior Telegram, Wausau Daily Record-Herald* and the *Wisconsin State Journal*. The Hurley Historical Society, the Ashland Historical Society and the Ironwood Carnegie Library provided important source material.

The Illustrated History of Pro Football, by Robert Smith, provided interesting historical information about the development of football and about some of the early players and coaches in the National Football League. Catherine Techtmann's book, *Rooted in Resources: Iron County, Wisconsin 1893-1993* provided historical and geographical details.

Thanks to Coach's players, peers and friends for their letters, which I took the liberty to quote. Special thanks to Bruce Fossum for his comments and insights used in the chapter, "The Tale of Two Seasons."

Thanks to Joe and Patricia Walsh, Eleanor McKeeman, Jackie Reid Dettloff, John Halbert and Nicholas Wood for their thoughts and proof reading; to Mark Stevens, Brian Toal, Mary Williams, Nicole Sperekas and Greg Borowski for their advice; to Gina Diliberti and Clark Graphics' Molly Carey for photo and cover assistance.

My wife, Eleanor, gets credit for the title *A Coach for all Seasons*, as well as for proof reading and for suggestions on the structure of the book.

There is no way I can thank my sister Maggie enough. Without her there would be no book. She is the genesis of the book, as her prodding finally got me writing. She did the research and typing. This is as much her book as it is mine.

CONTENTS

A COACH
FOR
ALL SEASONS

PROLOGUE

THIS IS THE STORY of a time, a place and a man. It is the story of a time — the second quarter of the twentieth century. It is not history, but a collection of vignettes of a time past and almost forgotten. It is the story of a place — northern Wisconsin, particularly the towns of Hurley and Ashland. It is not geography, but a description of how a unique place shaped a people. It is the story of a man —Roy E. Melvin. It is not a biography. It is the memories of a son.

My Dad was a coach, not just of football, basketball, baseball, track, or tennis, but a coach for all seasons. When my sister Maggie's first grade teacher asked her what her father's first name was, she remembers proudly saying, "Coach!"

She was startled at her teacher's retort, "No, that's his job. What does your Mother call him?"

Maggie quickly replied, "Mel"! Maggie knew she had given the wrong answer when she heard her teacher's frustrated mumble, "No! That's a nickname - 'Mel' for Melvin."

Maggie wanted to argue. It was her Dad and she knew his name. Fortunately she knew enough not to argue with the teacher. By the time she got home she ran into the house yelling, "Mom, what is Daddy's first name?"

She was shocked when Mother matter-of-factly said, "Roy ... Roy Earl Melvin." That was my sister's first memory of hearing Dad's real name. After all, everyone in town just called him Coach!

Although this book deals primarily with football and basketball, Dad and his peers also coached tennis, track and baseball or some combination of these five sports. Many would consider this a burden. In fact, it was an advantage! Many athletes played more than one sport, which allowed coaches to become very familiar with their individual talents, attitudes, strengths and weaknesses. They knew their players. The community's coach was highly respected, often admired, and occasionally loved. He significantly influenced many young men's lives.

Roy Melvin came to northern Wisconsin in the summer of 1923 to play professional baseball and stayed for twenty-eight years to teach school and coach high school sports. This book is a story of those years. It is a tribute to a father, and to the many other men who taught and coached in America's small towns. These men coached sports and prepared their players for life.

Coach Roy Melvin in the early 1930s

CHAPTER 1

THE MAKING OF A COACH
1923–1940

NO ONE BUT DAD HEARD THE FURNACE EXPLODE! He was found bleeding and blind. In his eleventh year as Coach at Hurley High School, his budding career seemed over. Or was it?

The doctor diagnosed no physical damage to the eyes, but Dad still couldn't see. Trauma was the culprit. The doctor said that only time would tell – maybe he would recover his sight, or maybe he wouldn't. For dad and mother it was the longest six months of their lives.

ACCIDENTS WERE NOT UNFAMILIAR to the Melvin family. The oldest child of John Melvin and Emma Thorpe, Roy Earl Melvin was born December 15, 1896 in Fish Creek, Door County, Wisconsin. He was part of Door County's large pioneer Claflin-Thorpe clan. His mother, Emma, was the granddaughter of the legendary Increase Claflin, the first permanent settler in Door County. Increase had eleven daughters and three sons. The Claflin girls were the only Caucasian women, so they became the foundation of many of the first families in Door County. Like many Door County men, Dad's mother's first husband, a fisherman, was one of many lost at sea.

Among the tall Melvin men, Roy was the runt of the family. His 6′ 2″ to 6′ 8″ uncles and father dwarfed him. At age twenty-one, Roy was just 5′ 9″ and 133 pounds. In the first decade of the twentieth century, young Roy learned reading, writing and arithmetic at the small elementary school in Fish Creek. His father was a fisherman in the spring, summer and fall and a lumberjack in the winter, so Dad learned the skills of swimming, sailing and chopping at an early age. Boxing, too, was a part of the fishing business. Every Friday night the sons of fishermen sold the catch of the day on the street corners. The best boxer got the best corner for selling fish. Roy's father knew that if his son was going to sell the family's fish he had to compensate for his son's average build with better than average boxing skills, so he taught him. Even at that early age, Dad's unusual athletic abilities were evident.

When Dad was fourteen the family moved across the waters of Green Bay to Marinette, Wisconsin, a much larger city. There he could attend high school and his father could continue his fishing business. Two years later, Dad left home and moved to landlocked Wausau, Wisconsin where he finished his last two years of high school. Since he knew no one in Wausau, he boarded out. To earn his room and board one of his jobs was turning cattle out to pasture in the early morning and driving them back in the evening. Like a cowboy, Dad rode a horse and carried a rifle to ward off the timber wolves that still ranged in northern Wisconsin. The next year the rest of the family moved to Wausau. Dad and his younger siblings all completed high school there.

The importance placed on education in the Melvin home was no surprise. His grandparents, Jacob and Maria Thorpe, started the first school in Egg Harbor, Wisconsin. They sent their two daughters, Lillian and Dad's mother, Emma, to training schools downstate and brought them home as teachers. Their first classes consisted of their siblings, their neighbors' children and a handful of Indian children. Dad's father was considered the family philosopher and storyteller. His mother, a teacher, later became a published music composer and poet.

While in Wausau, Dad learned to play tennis at the YMCA. He also participated in high school football and basketball, but because of his size saw limited action. During the time Dad played high school football there was no such thing as a forward pass. Because of his small size, he did get to play in a unique "pass play." The Wausau coach had leather straps sewn on Dad's jersey. When the team needed short yardage, he inserted him into the line-up. When the ball was snapped to Dad, two large teammates, one on each side of him, immediately grabbed the straps and literally threw Dad, with the ball, over the line of scrimmage. At that early age, Dad was ahead of his time! Was this the forerunner of today's forward pass?

When Dad graduated from Wausau High School he was again on his own. This time his dreams took him to Madison, Wisconsin, where he enrolled as a freshman at the University of Wisconsin. World War I interrupted his college life. Just a few days short of his twenty-first birthday, Dad enlisted in the United States Navy. He was assigned to naval aviation. He trained in radio communication at Harvard University. While in Boston he traveled the East Coast and played on the Harvard tennis team. After completing training, he flew reconnaissance missions in dirigibles and open cockpit bi-wing planes.

Gunner Roy in Pensacola, Florida

When Roy was discharged, a former baseball teammate at Madison and current baseball coach at River Falls Normal College convinced Dad to come to River Falls. There, he played baseball, basketball and football and completed his teaching certification in physical education. Roy then returned to the University of Wisconsin and, in the spring of 1923, graduated with a bachelor's degree in history.

Dad discovered baseball as a team sport when he arrived at the University of Wisconsin. He excelled in baseball. He played on the university baseball team for three years. During that same time, he also played on the Madison All Stars, a team that competed against the professional Reedsburg Nine led by Shoeless Joe Jackson. Jackson, and seven of his Chicago White Sox teammates, had gone to the Reedsburg professional club after the gambling debacle, the Black Sox Scandal of 1919.

When Dad finished college he actually had a major league contract offer from the Cincinnati Red Legs. Instead he headed north to Hurley, Wisconsin to play professional baseball. A top player could make good money playing on these small town professional teams. Some say better money than in the major leagues where the pay was low and the expenses (travel, lodging and food) were high. In 1923, the same year Dad started playing baseball in Hurley, the great Ty Cobb was making about $3,000 a year. At $50 a game, Dad made $1,800 for a twelve week summer season of three games each week. Quite a pay check for 1923!

Professional baseball was big in the northern Wisconsin and Michigan mining and lumbering towns. It wasn't unusual for the Northwestern Railroad line to put on special trains to take the players and fans to the few long distance games. On one railroad trip to Antigo, Wisconsin, over 300 fans bought $6.00 round trip train tickets to see their Hurley baseball team play.

Dad's forte was power hitting. To the fans that meant one thing – home runs! In his first game, played at the old Hurley Legion Field just south of Silver Street, he struck out three of his four times at bat and was roundly booed. He had been touted as a star and was the highest paid player on the team. He had to quickly turn things around or his summer employment would be prematurely over. During the next two games he hit two home runs over the ten-foot-high center field fence, some 410 feet away from home plate. These were reputed to be the only home runs ever hit over that portion of the fence. Dad had gone from star-to-bum-to-hero in just three games. As the *Iron County Miner* stated, "Melvin, third baseman, who came up from Madison with

Hoffman, handles himself like a real fastball player. He has a good arm and gets the ball away from him nice."

Full page ad from Montreal River Miner, 1923

AS A KID I KNEW THAT DAD HAD ACUTE EYESIGHT. When we would be out in the woods he could spot things I couldn't see. Some of my best memories are of grouse hunting with Dad around Island Lake. It was like walking through a tree cemetery. Mile after mile of twelve foot high tree stumps stood like dark grey sentinels. The silence was broken only by the drumming wings of the grouse. The tree stumps and the crisscrossing fire lanes were the only signs of human intrusion. When I first starting hunting with Dad I "hunted" without a gun. Later I carried an unloaded gun. Finally, I got to shoot.

One Sunday afternoon we were tramping down a fire lane when Dad stopped and whispered, "There's a grouse about a block and a half down the lane on the right-hand side."

Startled, I asked, "Where?"

"About the seventh fence post down. Can't you see its head just above the weeds?" Then he told me, "Walk ahead slowly and you'll probably flush the bird."

Although I still couldn't see the bird, I cautiously followed along the fence line, passing one post and then another. I still couldn't see the grouse's head. I began to think that Dad was seeing things!

When I approached the seventh fence post I was sure he was seeing things. There wasn't any bird. Suddenly, a grouse burst into the air. By the time I got settled down for the shot, the bird was long gone.

I was fourteen when I actually saw him hit a baseball. At that time he was managing the semi-pro Ashland City Team. The Ashland team had good pitchers. There was a young left-handed pitcher who really impressed me. Dad said, "Ah, he's good for this level of play but he can't prevail against good batters." Then he seemed to boast, "I could hit his pitches every time!" To me that seemed like a safe statement, considering Dad would never have to face this pitcher.

Toward the end of summer, the city team scheduled a traditional double header against the "old timers." The old timers were short of players so they asked Dad to play with them. Dad, now forty-nine, had not swung a bat for over ten years. After some coaxing he agreed to play, provided that I could run for him. I was excited, especially when I heard that the good left-handed pitcher would be pitching for the city team. Now Dad would have the chance to prove his "I could hit him every time" boast. In the two games, he batted nine times and got eight hits. I was convinced!

Before that 1923 baseball season ended, Mr. J. E. Murphy, Superintendent of the Hurley schools, offered Dad a job to teach and coach at Hurley High School. Twenty-six-year-old Roy, who had left small town America for university and military life, a baseball player who had come only for the summer, accepted and stayed. At the time Dad couldn't possibly have known how this decision would shape his life and the lives of so many young men.

JUST AS THAT ONE DECISION BEGAN TO SHAPE A MAN, the geography of the North Woods, with its rocky outcroppings, fresh water lakes, big trees, extreme winters and "red gold" deep underground, shaped a people.

The North Woods encompasses the land north and south of Lake Superior, including parts of Minnesota, Wisconsin and Michigan. From International Falls, Minnesota in the far northwest to Sault Sainte Marie, Michigan in the east, this southwest section of the Laurentian Plateau is part of the rocky core of North America.

On a modern day road map the North Woods is the land east of U.S. Highway 53 in Minnesota, north of U.S. Highway 10 in Wisconsin and all of the upper peninsula of Michigan. This was the land of the mythical Paul Bunyan and Babe, his

Blue Ox. This was the home of the Chippewa Indian Nation.

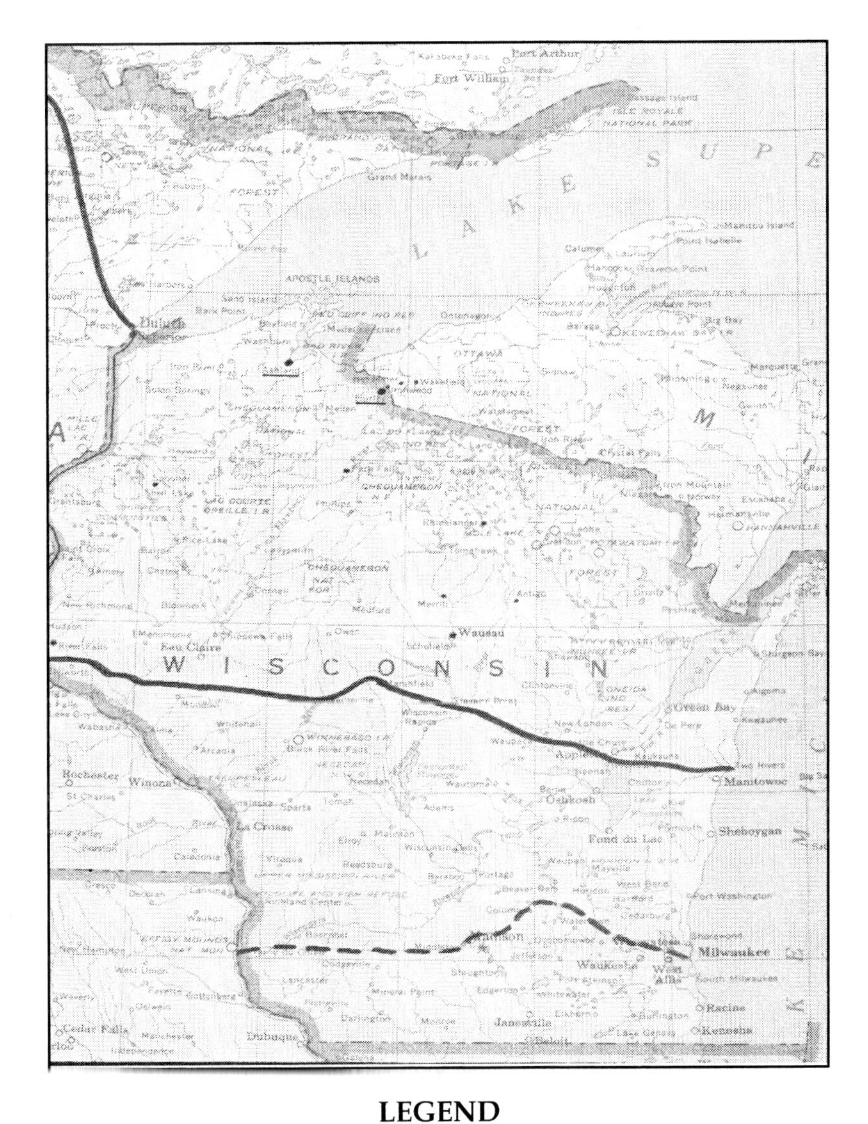

LEGEND

________ **North Woods' Boundary**

----------- **North-South All-Star Game Boundary**

Prior to 1840 this last remnant of the Northwest Territory was a total wilderness. Although a few came in search of furs, it was what lay beneath the land that brought those who stayed.

In the 1840s, copper was discovered in the Keweenaw Peninsula of Michigan and permanent mining settlements quickly dotted the landscape. For forty more years the rest of the North Woods remained wilderness. In 1880 two discoveries dramatically changed this area. In the process of laying down new railroad tracks, workers from the Lake Superior Ship Canal Railroad discovered iron ore on the west side of the Montreal River at the site of present day Hurley, Wisconsin. That same year a trapper, Richard Langford, discovered a chunk of red rock stuck in the roots of an overturned tree on the east side of the Montreal River near present day Bessemer, Michigan. This was the beginning of the iron boom on the Penokee Range, locally known as the Gogebic Range or just plain the "Range."

The ore in the Gogebic Range was rich and ran in large, deep veins along a twenty-five to thirty mile strip from Wakefield, Michigan to Iron Belt, Wisconsin. These mines were active from the early 1880s to the mid 1960s. The bulk of the ore mined in Wisconsin was shipped out of Ashland, Wisconsin, thirty-eight miles west of Hurley.

Tens of thousands of settlers poured into the North Woods, especially to the Gogebic Range. The first wave of settlers were U.S. born Irish, Scots and English who migrated west, first to Michigan to work in the copper mines and then, after iron ore was discovered, to the Gogebic Range. Many of these early settlers eventually moved on to the copper mines of Montana. Immigrants from Europe, especially from Scandinavia, Italy, Poland, Germany, and Great Britain, replaced them. Those who survived the arduous journey to this new world brought families and worked in the many underground iron ore mines. Regardless of their country of origin they had common aspirations and backgrounds. They were deeply religious, hard working and determined. They wanted to learn English. They wanted their children to be educated. They shared a common experience: they had left Europe for economic, political or religious reasons and came to start anew.

Growing up in Hurley in the 1930s, my world was filled with these first and second generation European immigrants. In the summer, when President FDR's Fireside Chats were broadcast, our yard would be packed with neighbors. We had one of the town's few radios, a Crosley, purchased for $50.00 in 1930. We opened up all the windows and turned the radio up high so that Roosevelt's resonant voice wafted over the intent adults and exuberant children. I don't remember what the president said, but even now I can feel the sense of confidence his voice instilled. I vividly remember the time after the broadcast. We would have a big backyard bonfire for a potato roast and lots of adult talk ... talk ... talk ... about the country's problems and solutions. Whenever someone said, "In the old country we did it this way," there would be an outcry of "Don't be foolish!" ... "We don't want to hear about the old country!" ... "We left the old country!"... "We're Americans now!" Since the old country meant Europe, I thought Europe must be a terrible place, one too awful to talk about.

Not all the people in Hurley were European immigrants. A second wave of settlers hit the North Woods in the 1890s. Lumberjacks migrated from Michigan, Maine and Canada to fell the big pine trees, exceeded in size only by the huge Douglas firs, redwood and sequoias. By 1888, two thousand woodsmen were in the Hurley area. The lumberjacks differed from the miners who came with families. Most of the lumberjacks were single men and lived in what was known as "jungle camps." Single, with money in their pockets, they came into town for booze, women and gambling.

In the short space of twenty years the North Woods was transformed from wilderness to boom towns. By 1890 four passenger railroads served the area: The Milwaukee Lakeshore, the Western, the Duluth, and the South Shore and Atlantic. Dozens of thriving communities had bustling main streets with boarding houses, a general store, saloons and a post office. On the second floor of many of these buildings were offices for realtors, doctors, dentists and attorneys, as well as the town meeting hall and numerous brothels. The wide treeless main streets of these early northern towns reflected the different lifestyles of the miners, the lumberjacks and the big city investors and visitors. Further west, Ashland and Superior, Wisconsin became major shipping ports. During the 1890s Ashland was one of the largest cities in Wisconsin with over forty docks from which iron ore, lumber and lumber products were shipped.

By the early 1920s logging activities ended. Hard times hit the lumberjacks. Many were forced to leave; others homesteaded, took wives, started families and settled permanently in the area.

When Dad arrived in Hurley in 1923 the frontier atmosphere of the North Woods was waning. By the end of that decade Iron County, Wisconsin had a population of 10,261. The "red gold" beneath the land and the "white gold" of the towering pines had brought a rich mix of peoples and cultures to the area, forever changing the landscape of the North Woods.

To people not from Hurley, Hurley was famous as one of northern Wisconsin's three H's: Hurley, Hayward and Hell. Of the three, they say Hurley was the toughest. Hurley's infamous Silver Street, a four block stretch lined with taverns where booze, women and gambling flowed freely, was really no different from the main streets of most mining towns. Silver Street just lasted longer – a lot longer.

Hurley's Silver Street looking east towards Ironwood Michigan

Dad arrived during the height of the Prohibition Era and Hurley was a bootleggers' paradise. The *Milwaukee Journal* details a 1921 incident when federal agents "shot up a booze caravan of twenty-one autos and trucks bound from Milwaukee to Hurley." There were frequent raids by federal agents. Slot machines would be loaded on to trucks, women scampered out of town, the town closed up tight for days. When the "all clear" was sounded, the slot machines and women streamed back.

Years later, in the 1950s, when my brother Tom's Superior Cathedral High School class traveled to Hurley to participate in the area music festival, the Cathedral students were warned not to go to the ill-reputed Silver Street. Social Tom, quick to seek a little money and adventure, organized tours of the infamous Silver Street, to the amusement of those of us who knew Hurley as home and to the consternation of the nuns.

To the people who lived there, Hurley was a good town. They knew another side of Hurley from that reported in the newspapers and painted in Edna Ferber's novel, *Come and Get It*. They knew a town peopled by first and second generation immigrants who worked hard, valued education and loved their sports.

One of the most influential men in Hurley's history was J. E. Murphy. Like Dad, Mr. Murphy had come to Hurley right out of college. He came to teach, soon became high school principal and then, for fifty years, school superintendent. To the immigrant parents, who saw education as the key to their children's future, J. E. Murphy was next to God. He didn't disappoint the parents. Graduates of Hurley High School had one of the highest percentages in the state for attendance and graduation from college. Dad was as proud of this achievement as of any of the successes of his athletic teams.

Superintendent Murphy and high school Principal Connors also didn't disappoint their teachers. Dad considered working with Mr. Murphy and Mr. Connors a privilege. He totally embraced their philosophy expressed in the Hurley High School motto: **"The purpose of our high school is to teach pupils to do better what they will be called upon to do later in life."** Dad was deeply influenced by Mr. Murphy's educational principles as expressed by Mr. Connors on the occasion of Mr. Murphy's twenty-five years in Hurley. "It is not the province of the teacher to teach only the three R's, but to teach charity.... It is not the function of the public schools to pick out the leaders and educate them to lead the rest, but to educate and elevate the level and standing of all humanity."

In Hurley Roy had the support of administration, parents, and the entire community. Many years later Dad talked about that support when he explained:

> Support from the fans and moral backing is essential - that is part of the secret of Hurley's success. Hurley is a great mining town and when I coached there the miners, over half the population, followed the team all over. During an afternoon grid game in Ironwood, the miners left work at 3:00. They took off and went to the state tournament in 1943. The miners were so close to the team that many of them took the part of cheerleaders.

The community was much larger than just the city of Hurley. It was the entire Gogebic Range. Within fourteen miles there were four principal towns: Ironwood, Bessemer, and Wakefield in Michigan, and Hurley in Wisconsin. Although four separate towns, in two states, with four high schools fiercely competitive in sports, the Range was, in spirit and outlook, one community. When one of Dad's football players, Johnny Alice, died, not only did the entire Hurley High School student body attend his funeral, but the Range football teams from Ironwood, Bessemer and Wakefield did as well.

Sports, especially baseball and football, were big entertainment. Green Bay, Wisconsin and Duluth, Minnesota were charter members of the National Football League. Players from the North Woods, including Curly Lambeau, George Gipp, Ernie Nevers, John Hancock, Johnny McNalley (popularly known as Johnny Blood), Bronko Nagurski and Al "Tuffy" Leemans, are numbered among the greatest players in football history. These greats were followed by others, including Bruce Smith, Teddy Gentile, Elroy "Crazy Legs" Hirsch, Dominic Moselle, Harry "Bud" Grant, Chuck Yderstad, Dave Suminski, Jim Otto, and Alex Webster.

In fact, of the approximate 250 players currently in the NFL Hall of Fame, nine got their football start in the North Woods. Of these nine, seven started their careers prior to 1950.

This was the sports milieu in which Dad began to hone his coaching strategies and techniques that eventually would become legendary on the Gogebic Range. The *Ironwood Times* publicly introduced Dad to the Range with these words:

> Roy Melvin who has been appointed physical [education] director of the Lincoln High School in Hurley, is a graduate of the University of Wisconsin and River Falls Normal [Teacher's College] in both of which schools he took courses in physical education.
>
> At the Normal School Melvin played quarterback and was a member of the team which took the Normal championship three years in succession. He also has had experience in other sports, and Hurley people feel that if he knows as much about football and basketball as he does about baseball, they will be more than satisfied.
>
> Twenty-four men reported to Melvin yesterday when he issued the first football call of the year. Twelve of the men who reported are veterans and won their letters last year. Regular practice was slotted to get underway tonight.

It is amazing to me that eighty years later he is still fondly remembered. Just a few years ago my sister was poking around in the Hurley Historical Society Museum when she ran into a Hurley High School alumnus who queried, "Are you Coach Melvin's daughter?"

Surprised that she looked enough like Dad that she could be recognized by a total stranger, she blurted out, "Yes, do I look like my Dad?" She didn't, but word had spread that Coach Melvin's daughter was at the museum.

When she asked him if he had played for Dad, he smiled and replied, "No, I was the brainy type, but we all loved your Dad. There wasn't a dry eye in this town when your Dad left."

Near the end of Dad's first year of coaching, it was evident that he had found a niche. The *Bessemer Herald* newspaper praised him in these words:

> Coach Roy Melvin has made a good record, since he took up the athletic reins at Hurley High last fall. His football and basketball teams have been among the best in the history of Hurley athletics. His football eleven tied Bessemer High last fall and his basketball outfit has won two games from the locals—performances which are rare indeed in Bessemer-Hurley contests. Fans also have had an opportunity to see Melvin display his prowess in baseball and basketball since he came to Hurley. That town sure gained in athletic prestige since Melvin got there.

WHEN DAD STARTED COACHING IN THE FALL OF 1923, he had a lot to learn, not the least of which was his competition. His three major Wisconsin competitors, the two Superior high schools and Ashland High, were significantly larger than

Hurley High.

He must have had a real shock when he found out the situation with his competitors across the border in Michigan. It wasn't their enrollment size; it was the state's eligibility rules. In the 1920s a high school student in Michigan could play sports regardless of his age or the number of years he had previously played, as long as he was currently enrolled.

Athletes from Ironwood, Bessemer and Wakefield played well into their twenties, playing five, six, seven or more years. They would enroll in high school in the fall, play football, drop out of school to work in the mines for eight to nine months, re-enter high school the next fall and compete in football year after year. This meant that strong, mature and experienced Michigan men competed against Hurley boys. Tough competition, indeed! Some of these Michigan men played football on both the city's high school and semi-pro teams. Dad told me that he would coach against these players on Saturday afternoon and play against them in Sunday's semi-pro game.

Under these circumstances, why would Hurley schedule games against these Michigan schools? The answer was simple. They wouldn't have had much of a season if they didn't, because there weren't a sufficient number of Wisconsin schools within a reasonable travel distance. Fortunately, by the late 1930s, the eligibility rules of the two states became more equitable.

DAD'S EARLY TEAMS AT HURLEY weren't the best he ever coached, but, I believe he liked them the best, or, at least, he talked about them more than any of his other teams. Although I never met or even saw any of them, except Ed

Sybedon, Mario Giannunzio and Tom "Five Yard" Kirby, I feel I know them: Tommy Hunt, the Wilcox brothers, Bob "Mushy" Reible, Gil Trier and so many others.

Dad told stories about the early years: the third season when the last three football games were cancelled because of early snow storms and cold weather; line plunging Kirby who carried tacklers on his back over the goal line; the 1928 determined band of Midgets who gave Hurley its first victory over Bessemer in ten years; the 1930 gridiron squad that vanquished Ashland for the first time in twenty years.

Coach, Melvin with his first football team – 1923
Front Row: Pedri, Hunt, Giannunzio, Menestrena, Gertz, Draver Middle Row: Oddino, Pawlicki, L. Wlcox, Calvi, Gersich, C. Wilcox, Meade, Pecotte, Sturgal Top Row: Coach Melvin, Thomas, Gygi, Trier, Ruggles, Saari, Rosenberger, Stonemark, Schmagner, manager Aspinwall

Coach Melvin with his first Hurley High basketball team, 1923-24
Top Row: Coach, Oddino, Gygi, Saari, Manager Aspinwall
Bottom Row: Sybeldon, Calvi, Pedri, Hunt, Wicox

BY THE 1930s Dad had established a solid reputation. On the Range he was respected and admired. In Hurley, I don't believe I would be in error to say he was beloved.

Highly regarded as a teacher and coach, Dad did other things to endear himself to the community. Every summer he took a large contingent of boys camping for a week. He bought basketball shoes for those players who couldn't afford them. He encouraged boys and girls alike to enroll in college and made that possible for dozens and dozens of his players by helping them get financial assistance, scholarships or jobs.

Dad also endeared himself to a fourth grade teacher. Lucille Fitzgerald was an Irish girl from Ashland who had graduated from Superior Normal College. Before coming to Hurley, she had taught one year in Cornell, Wisconsin and five years in the Chicago area. Roy and Lou married in August of 1931. A year later I was born. By the time the new decade arrived, the Melvin family had grown to five: Tom was born in 1937 and Maggie in 1940.

Roy and his bride, Lucille, 1931 **Tom, Maggie and Stu, 1945**

Coach's Family

In his first ten years at Hurley, Dad established high school athletic programs in football, basketball, tennis and track. In the summer he coached the American Legion baseball team. In his first year at Hurley twenty-four boys came out for football. Ten years later there were sixty boys on the team. Dad had a good eye for athletic ability and was persuasive in getting boys to play two or more sports. Many of his best athletes were stars in a number of sports. In 1929 the Hurley and Ironwood Kiwanis Clubs sponsored a first ever Range track meet. About 150 athletes from Hurley, Ironwood, Bessemer, Wakefield, Anvil and Ontonagon high schools competed. In this first track meet Coach's boys won seven of the eight team trophies and fifteen of the thirty individual medals. The Hurley lads scored a total of 91.5 points, only nine points less that all the other schools combined.

The 1930 Hurley High School year book, *Spyke,* in its dedication to Coach said:

> When Coach Melvin came to Hurley High School, the athletic department was a haphazardly organized branch of the school. Since then, the department has grown every year, with the result that, where formerly there was one boy participating actively in athletics, there are now four. The physical training of the student body as a whole has developed into a truly integral part of the school curriculum.
>
> Mr. Melvin has done something of even greater value for the students, however. He has, in his work and in his associations with the "fellows," tried not only to produce winning teams for Hurley High School, but also to develop character and a sense of sportsmanship to the highest possible degree. The clean, hard play seen on the gridiron, cinder-path, and basketball floor is tangible evidence of his successful effort to accomplish this end. The coach's popularity and the niche he occupies in the esteem of the students are the direct result of his keen desire at all times to do the thing that is fair and square.

THE HURLEY HIGH SCHOOL TEAM NAME was the "Midgets." In 1930 a 110-pound, 5′1″ freshman "midget" entered Hurley High School. Many considered Teddy Gentile the mightiest of the Midgets. Years later Dad called Teddy, "Pound for pound and inch for inch, the greatest athlete he had ever seen!" And he had seen many a great athlete in his sixty years of playing and coaching. Teddy starred in football, basketball and track during his four years at Hurley High School. He went on to play at Superior State Teacher's College, starring in football for three years.

Dad was in the Superior stadium for Teddy's first college game as a sophomore. Superior State was up against powerful Concordia College from Kansas. At half time Superior was down three or four touchdowns. Dad went into the Superior locker room and suggested to Ted Whereatt, the Superior State coach, that he put Teddy into the game. Coach Whereatt responded by saying, "Why Mel, he's so small! How would he defend against their big ends?" Concordia had a large team with a couple of players who later played in the National Football League, including Ken Strong, a future inductee into the National Football League Hall of Fame.

Dad replied, "You can't do any worse." It was hard to argue against that logic. Teddy played the second half. Superior played Concordia College evenly in the second half with each team scoring one touchdown. Teddy played every quarter of every game after that. Very soon after that game the newspaper started calling "half pint Gentile... a difference maker" and lauding him as "five foot two—with eyes of black for the opposition."

I never saw Teddy play football or basketball. I played, however, in numerous football and basketball games in which he officiated. He was, by far, the quickest and fastest individual on the field or court. He could run up the basketball court backwards faster than the players could run forward, then stop and be at full speed forward with his first step.

Dad had a strong bond with Teddy. Teddy played four years for Dad. Dad was instrumental in Teddy going to Superior State Teachers College. Teddy later returned to Hurley and was Dad's assistant coach. The closeness between

Dad and his players was not unusual. Dad formed strong relationships with many of his players – relationships that lasted a lifetime. But something happened in Teddy's senior year at Hurley that forged a very special bond between Dad and Teddy.

Mom, Dad and I had just returned home from a Christmas with Grandma and Grandpa. The house was cold when we got home so Mom and I went to the neighbors and Dad went to our basement to stoke the furnace and warm up the house. He opened the furnace door. The fire was out. Dad lit a match to start the fire. Within moments, there was a terrible explosion. The furnace door flew off its hinges. With particles of dust and soot cinders driven into his face and eyes, Dad crawled out of the house and was found in the snow by the neighbors. Long uncertain days followed. Blinded, his future seemed bleak. The headlines in the *Ironwood Daily Globe* read, **ROY MELVIN HURT IN AN EXPLOSION.** The article continued:

> Severe injury to the eyes was suffered by Coach Roy Melvin of Lincoln High School yesterday afternoon when the draft door of the furnace at his home on Magnetic Street blew off. Mr. Melvin was temporarily blinded, but is not expected to suffer permanent injury to the eyes, said the attending physician today.
>
> The Melvin family went to Ashland for the Christmas holiday and the accident occurred when Mr. Melvin was starting a fire in the furnace. An accumulation of gas is believed to have caused the explosion.

Almost immediately Ironwood's Coach Mark Almli stepped in to direct Hurley's holiday basketball practice sessions. Despite the fierce rivalry between the two schools, this show of support personifies the unity of the Range community.

Amazingly, with bandages covering his blinded eyes, Dad resumed his teaching and coaching duties in a few weeks. The *Ironwood Daily Globe's* account of the first game after the accident is equally amazing:

> The Hurley team was directed from the bench by Coach Roy Melvin, who sat on the bench with his eyes bandaged and listened to the account of the game. After the game you would have sworn that Melvin saw the contest, for he knew all of the details even to the point of how many shots each player took and the mistakes they made. Melvin, more than ever, demonstrated that he has a wonderful basketball mind. Any man who can get such a mental picture as he did from a mere description of the game knows basketball.

It was team captain, Teddy Gentile, who gave Dad play by play descriptions of what was happening on the floor. Teddy was his eyes.

I was too young to remember any of this. I really didn't know about it until years later when I asked Dad, "How long does it take to become a good coach?"

He said, "About eight to ten years."

I asked, "Why?"

"Well, it takes about that long to experience most of the important aspects of coaching." Then he paused and added, "But I became a complete coach the year I was blind." He told me the story: the accident ... not knowing if he'd ever coach again ... about Teddy. Then he said, "Because I couldn't see, I learned to think!" He had to learn to analyze situations that he couldn't see, a skill which served him well the rest of his coaching career. I believe this analytical ability made him a great coach in so many sports.

On that winter day an accident that seemingly ended a budding career was really the birth of "The Wizard of the North Woods." Dad's coaching apprenticeship was over!

IN 1936, HURLEY'S PROFESSIONAL BASEBALL TEAM DISBANDED and Dad's baseball playing days were over. The next summer Dad applied for work at the iron ore mine in Montreal, Wisconsin. A few days later, while discussing his application with the superintendent of mines, Dad was chastised for even thinking about being a miner. After all, he was a teacher and teachers didn't work in mines. The superintendent, however, had a different work proposal for Dad. It seems that the superintendent had, for some time, been thinking about establishing a summer recreation program in the mining communities of Hurley, Gile, Pence, Cary and Montreal. He asked Dad to prepare a plan and budget for such a program. Dad's plans were approved and he not only implemented the plan but supervised playgrounds in each of the five towns for the rest of his years in Hurley. These playgrounds were hubs of indoor and outdoor activities including tennis, outdoor basketball, baseball, volleyball, horseshoes, dart games, archery, jump ropes, folk dancing, storytelling and other organized games. In addition to providing recreational activities for boys and girls from five to fifteen, the program provided Dad the chance to observe and teach pre-high school boys in various sporting activities.

He promoted and supported the formation of the Michigan-Wisconsin Conference. The conference, started in 1937, consisted of the Wakefield Cardinals, Bessemer

Speed Boys, and Ironwood Red Devils from Michigan, and the Hurley Midgets and Ashland Purgolders (later known as the Oredockers) from Wisconsin. Coach believed playing in an athletic conference was important because it provided goals for his teams. He considered winning a conference championship a top priority and always stressed conference games. There was considerable balance within the league, with only Ironwood significantly larger than the other four schools.

BY THE LATE 1930s DAD HAD ESTABLISHED A REPUTATION as a storyteller. Years later the Wisconsin High School Coaches Association decided to give a trophy to the coach who told the best stories at their annual coaches' meeting. One coach, however, was disqualified from trophy competition because he was considered a professional storyteller. In honor of the "professional storyteller" the trophy was named the Melvin Traveling Trophy. The annual winner's name was engraved on the trophy and the winner got to keep the trophy until the next annual meeting.

When Dad talked about the trophy and its theme, "slinging the bull," I thought he was joking and it was all "bull." When Dad retired the trophy was permanently given to him. The next time I was home for a visit, I saw the trophy and was amazed. It was a golfer, but instead of a golf club the golfer was swinging a twelve-inch bull by the horns.

Roy was a frequent public speaker at many community events. On one occasion he took the podium and realized he didn't have a watch. He asked if anyone in the audience had one. Someone laughingly called out, "Coach you don't need a watch, you need a calendar!"

Talkative and affable as he was, he could spend lots of time seemingly doing nothing. On Sunday he would drive us to church, and sit in the car, with no radio, no CD player - just his own thoughts. He was always thinking, always observing.

DAD OBSERVED A CYCLICAL PATTERN to the athletic talent in high school. At Hurley and later in Ashland this cycle was approximately four years. In 1938 the cycle peaked and Hurley had one of its better years with a 5-2 record in football and 10-5 in basketball. Naturally its two losses in football were to Ironwood and Bessemer.

The next season, following the cyclical pattern, was a poor one. In fact, it was one of the poorest years, record-wise, that Coach had in his twenty-eight years at Hurley and Ashland. However, on the bright side, Dominic Moselle and Don Dick entered Hurley High School as freshmen. A new cycle was starting. Prospects were looking up.

AS THE DECADE OF THE 1930s WANED, prospects were also looking up for the country. The worldwide economic crisis known as the Great Depression had consumed most of the 1930s. Before the nationwide depression hit, the demise of the lumbering industry had already propelled the North Woods' area into a recession. The depression only deepened the hard times. The drop in steel production further hurt the mining economics of the Gogebic Range. During the 1930s city populations and school enrollments on the Range declined.

By the end of the decade signs hinted at an economic upturn. The nationwide increase in economic activity was reflected in increased mining activity in the area. In the late 1930s Hurley High School committed to building a new basketball gym with the same floor plan as Dodd Gym in Ashland, built a few years earlier. Hurley's gym was completed in the summer of 1942. These two gyms had full size courts, large seating capacity and high ceilings with modern lighting.

As the new decade began, optimism was in the air. A hint of optimism even surrounded the 1940 Hurley – Ironwood football match-up. For years there had been a fierce sports rivalry between these two towns.

DAD EXPERIENCED BEING ON THE LOSING END of many match-ups with Michigan schools, especially the Ironwood Red Devils. This only fueled the rivalry between the two schools - a rivalry that extended back for years, interrupted only for a few years after the famous disputed 1920 game. The *Ironwood Times* details that legendary game:

> With some eight to ten minutes left to play and Hurley leading by a count of 6-0, the result of a touchdown by a brilliant run of end Sullivan, the Ironwood High School eleven was called off the field Saturday afternoon when a brawl started on the sidelines. The fight threatened to involve numerous spectators of both Hurley and Ironwood.
>
> Declaring that under the circumstances he could not permit his team to continue to play, Moss [the Ironwood coach] ordered his team to return to Ironwood and the game was forfeited to Hurley, 1 to 0.

Apparently poor officiating (a not uncommon occurrence in those days) was at the root of the problem. The newspaper quoted Hurley's Coach Lankey's response to this situation. "On behalf of the Hurley school and players, I wish to congratulate the Ironwood players in their clean sportsmanship. We've [Hurley High School] decided it's best for both schools not to meet anymore in sports events."

After a few years, competition between the two schools resumed. The Ironwood Red Devils were always the victor. As a kid I had recurring nightmares of being chased by swarms of red devils! But in 1940, for the first time since the disputed game twenty years earlier, Hurley was on a par with Ironwood. The Hurley Midgets, and they were midgets compared with Ironwood, were given a reasonable chance to win. The game ended in a 6-6 tie. The *Ironwood Daily Globe's* headlines **LIGHT MIDGET ELEVEN REALLY EARNED WIN** told the story; the reporter filled in the details:

> A fluke play deprived a brilliant, gallant Hurley High School eleven of a well earned victory this afternoon on the Hurley gridiron. Late in the last period Peterson [Ironwood] threw a wild pass down near the 20 yard line, a Hurley player batted the ball and as it bounced around Bogan [Ironwood], a substitute back, grabbed the ball and squirmed through several players to score.
>
> Hurley hit on the first half on a nice pass to Tomasin from Thomas. Throughout the game the Midgets out-fought and outplayed the bigger Red Devil team and staved off a long march in the fourth period by stopping Taylor on the one foot line
>
> It was a heart breaker for the Hurley fans and Midget players. The fans had visions of the first win in about 20 years after the long march was halted short of the goal line and the players could sense they had the Red Devils badly upset as the game neared its end.
>
> Coach Roy Melvin almost turned the trick of beating Ironwood with most of his backfield men

> on the sideline with bad injuries. Players were handling positions they never handled before and the third string backfield was in the game when the Midgets scored their touchdown.
>
> Castagna, Captain, and Moselle, Bugni, Hoeft, Nechak — oh, just about everyone — played great ball for Hurley.

This game typified the frustrations Dad endured at Hurley High School and later at Ashland High School because of his football players' lack of size and his teams' lack of depth. How many games did his teams lose in the fourth quarter by being ground down by opponent's superior size and depth?

1938 BROUGHT A CHANGE that shaped the next few decades of Wisconsin high school basketball. The WIAA, the governing body of Wisconsin high school athletics, changed the format of the state basketball tournament from three classes, based on school size, to a one class, single elimination tournament. No longer divided by enrollment, all schools would now compete in a single state championship. The first year of the classless, sudden death state tournament, a small North Wood's team, the Rhinelander Hodags, led by the great Johnny Kotz, won the 1939 state championship.

With the new gyms, the elimination of the center jump rule and now the single state wide tournament, basketball emerged to challenge football as the king of sports in northern Wisconsin.

COACH'S EIGHTEEN YEARS OF TEACHING AND COACHING EXPERIENCE were ready to pay off. The very limitation imposed by coaching at a small high school honed his innate skills. The lack of prior coaching experience meant he had to start with what he knew as a player and learn from there. Having no assistants meant he had to work with every individual on the squad. He got to know his players personally; he knew their strengths and weaknesses. Even being the trainer added to his skill and gave him opportunities before the game for little private talks with individual players. Having small players and few reserves meant he had to find better ways to play the game.

He couldn't be successful coaching in the tradition of such big school coaches as Jack Kraemer and Harry Conley. He had to have different philosophies, systems and strategies. That took time. Now he was posed for victory.

Typical football scene of the 1920's

Roy as a college basketball player

Roy as a college football player

CHAPTER 2

FOOTBALL AND BASKETBALL, YESTERDAY AND TODAY

IN THE BEGINNING OF THE TWENTIETH CENTURY there was no NFL, no NBA, no TV, no Super Bowl, no March Madness, and no ABC Wide World of Sports. There was football, basketball and baseball. By the second quarter of the twentieth century football and basketball were played by tens of thousands of high school players. The causal observer might think that there is little difference between football and basketball of yesterday and today. That perception is far from the facts. To understand how the games have developed and changed enter the time capsule of pre-1950.

American football roots go back many centuries. Those to whom a world without football is unfathomable might fantasize that God created football. A disproportionate number of these believers lived in small town America. God, however, is God. Football was just king! American football evolved from the English game of rugby. The further back in time you go, the more football resembles rugby.

By 1900 football had started its evolutionary development. The playing fields and rules moved toward standardization. Protective equipment emerged. The football itself started its long evolutionary journey: from round to oval ... to its current pointed "bullet-shape." The football was made of leather panels with an inflatable rubber inside which was an imitation of a pig's bladder - hence the name "pigskin."

By the 1910s the rules finally settled on eleven players per team. Substitutions were severely restricted and once a player was removed he could not return to the playing field during that half. The scoring system established six points for a touchdown, one point for the point after the touchdown, three points for a field goal, and two points for a safety. Running the ball, picking it up and advancing, with or without pushing, was the only method of moving the ball. Forward passing of any kind was not permitted.

To put the ball into play without the free-for-all melee of rugby's scrum method, a neutral zone, called the line of scrimmage, was created. A play began with teams facing each other at this line. A system of downs evolved. Initially a team had three downs to move the ball five yards. This soon changed to four downs to advance ten yards. Only four players were permitted in the backfield and, contrary to today's rules, these four could move before the ball was snapped.

Although football, by the 1920s, was still a running game, a limited type of passing crept into the game. *The Illustrated History of Pro Football* describes the pass itself in these words:

"It could be thrown only within five yards, laterally, of the point at which the ball was snapped. So the field had to be marked both ways - laterally as well as longitudinally - at five-yard intervals so officials could enforce this rule. These markings made the field look like a true gridiron, divided, lattice-style, in five-yard squares to form the grid." Later rule changes eliminated the need for longitudinal lines. Today the football field looks less like a grid, but it is still called the gridiron.

If a pass was thrown and the ball went out-of-bounds, possession of the ball went to the defense at the point where the ball crossed the out-of-bounds boundary. Because of this, a pass usually wasn't thrown until fourth down and frequently was used in lieu of a punt to pin the opponents in the "coffin corner."

As passing rules were liberalized the ball's shape evolved from egg shape to the modern bullet shape. These ball changes facilitated the forward pass.

Sometime in the 1920s the huddle was introduced. Offensive and defensive formations emerged. Linemen assumed a three or four point stance. Only one back could be in motion prior to the snap from center. Substitutions were still highly restricted and permitted only when the ball was dead.

In the early years the ball was put into play at the point where the last play ended. When the ball was put into play close to the sidelines there wasn't room for the normal formation line-ups so strong side and short side formations developed. Some of these were so extreme that all the players were lined up either to the right or left of the center. To correct this, the rule makers introduced "hash marks." These were lines parallel to the sidelines. If the previous play ended between the hash mark and the sideline the ball was put in play from the hash mark. Over time hash marks were moved inward. By 1950 they were approximately twelve or fifteen yards from the sideline. Today the hash marks are in direct line of the goal posts, contributing to the strategy of kicking field goals instead of punting. Punting as a defensive or offensive strategy diminished. Today more and more games are played in which field goals are the only score.

By far the most significant rule change influencing high school football was the series of "free substitution" rules leading to unrestricted substitution. Prior to the 1950s substitutions occurred only when the referee's whistle blew the ball dead. That meant only at the beginning of each quarter, at time outs, when the ball carrier went out-of-bounds, when points were scored or when the ball changed hands. The net effect was players played longer because they played both offense and defense and kickers were real players. Contrary to what one might think, this restricted substitution actually helped the smaller high schools as the larger schools couldn't fully utilize their greater depth. Since the 1950s football rules have permitted more and more substitution until we now have unrestricted and unlimited substitutions.

The essence of football is blocking and tackling. Rules governing these two aspects profoundly affect the nature of the game. In pre-1950 football, offensive players couldn't use their hands. That meant no pushing, pulling or holding. To prevent illegal blocking, players were actually taught to grab hold of their own jersey with both hands when attempting to block an opponent. Good blocking required using your whole body, getting appropriate position and making body contact. Blocking rules and their interpretations have so changed that today we have offensive linemen standing up on the snap of the ball, grabbing hold of their opponent, holding on as long as they can and then pushing the opponent, hopefully down.

Many football coaches looked for ways to take advantage of existing rules or new rule changes. Dad was no exception. I was always fascinated by Dad's stories of how he used the rules to his team's advantage. One year he sewed brown leather patches on the elbows of the backs' uniforms. Then, whenever a back was involved in a fake hand-off, the back would cross his arms. To the opposing defense those brown patches on the elbows looked like the ball and added to the success of a fake play.

Another year, when the school band and the team both had orange uniforms, Dad had the band stand shoulder-to-shoulder on the sideline. At an opportune time Dad called for a play to be run to the sideline opposite of the band, with an end drifting to the band's sideline. On the next play the ball was passed to the end who, unguarded and blending in with the band, ran for an unobstructed touchdown. Obviously this play worked only at home games and only once a game, but it showed Dad's imagination.

Occasionally Dad actually instructed a receiver to run out-of-bounds behind the players' bench, and then back on the field to receive a pass.

Over time the rules were changed and these trick plays were passé, but imaginative coaches still looked for loopholes in the prevailing rules to improve their teams' chances to win

IF GOD CREATED FOOTBALL then man created basketball. This truly American game started, we are told, in a barnyard. It quickly moved indoors. Court size, ceiling heights, lighting and other physical characteristics of the facility were totally dependent on the "room" that was used as a gym. Even in the 1940s gym characteristics varied greatly from school to school. Of the school gyms Dad coached in only Hurley, Ashland and Wakefield had what could be defined as modern gyms. These three gyms had full size courts, plenty of space around the out-of-bounds lines, high ceilings, and good lighting. Every other gym lacked one or more of these features.

Teams even had special offenses and defenses to compensate or take advantage of each gym's unique features. Games in Ashland's old gym were unforgettable. It had a balcony overhanging the west side of the playing court which made shooting from that side impossible. For play in this gym Coach's defensive strategy was simple: hold the opponent's ball handler on the west side of the court and trap him in the corner.

Basketball rules were more standard than gyms. By the 1930s scoring had settled to two points for a basket and one point for each free throw. Prior to 1950, three point shots and bonus free throws didn't exist. A player was allowed three fouls and was ejected when he committed his fourth foul. A fouled team had the option to take the ball out of bounds. By the 1940s the rules permitted a player one additional foul before being eliminated from the game.

A team had ten seconds to cross the center line. The dribbler had to have his dribbling hand on top of the ball and could take only one step after picking up the ball. Once a pivot foot was established you could not drag or lift that foot. The rules governing traveling, double dribbling and dragging the pivot foot were enforced and violations meant a loss of ball possession.

The interpretation of rules supported defensive position. Pre-1950 rules concerning contact between a defensive and offensive player penalized the offensive player with a foul if the defensive player occupied a position of three feet or more from the offensive player and attempted to maintain that position. All other body contact, except when going after a rebound or loose ball, was a foul against the defense. Pushing, holding, elbowing, and hitting were taboo. They resulted in fouls and, in extreme cases, ejection from the game. If players did then, what basketball players do now, the starting five would probably have fouled out by the end of the first quarter. Back then, the game was "clean." If Coach's players got too physical in practice, he cautioned them: "Basketball is not a contact sport. If you want contact, take up boxing, wrestling or football."

Even simple rule changes can have a material impact on game strategy. Well into the second half of the twentieth century basketball had no shot clock. The advent of the shot clock rule eliminated the concept of stalling. Most would applaud this. Just holding the ball was boring. On the other hand, interesting offensive uses of the stall, like the semi- stall or four corner offense, just vanished. Furthermore, coaches work on "good shot choices," and the shot clock is counter productive to this concept. It encourages shooting, whether in position or not. The advent of the shot clock rule actually gave the defense a huge advantage. It's a lot easier to defend a player against getting a good shot when you only have to defend for a very limited time. This advantage frequently seems overlooked by most modern coaches. Basketball today is more an offensive than defensive game.

The center jump rule, in effect until the late 1930s, was by far the most significant rule in basketball. The center jump rule called for a jump at center after every point was scored. In high school basketball the team with the tallest players or highest jumpers had a huge advantage because they had the ball most of the time. Since large high schools usually had taller players, they dominated high school basketball. Basketball was a low scoring, plodding and actionless contest. Why? When the smaller team finally got the ball, they wouldn't shoot until they had a sure shot. Sometimes a whole quarter was played without an attempted shot. No wonder the gyms were small and the crowds smaller.

In the late 1930s the center jump rule was eliminated. A new type of basketball emerged. Now a center jump was only used to put the ball in play at the beginning of each half and when ball possession could not be determined. At last the little schools had a chance and they took it with a vengeance. Dad occasionally joked that a lot of "good" coaches in large high schools retired after the elimination of the center jump.

THE LITTLE SCHOOLS weren't actually so little except by today's standards. These were four year high schools with enrollments between 300-500 students. A percentage of these students lived on farms and were not available for high school athletic teams. Of the schools mentioned in this book, Hurley, Ashland, Superior East, Bessemer, Wakefield, Rhinelander, Merrill, Antigo and Marshfield were about equal in size (350-450 total students) and DePadua (Parochial School in Ashland) and Park Falls were slightly smaller. Only Ironwood, Superior Central and Wausau high schools had larger enrollments. All of these schools had one coach for all sports and many had no assistants.

A typical high school football player averaged 150-160 pounds. A player more than two hundred pounds was rare.

Hurley and Ashland teams frequently had first string players weighing one hundred thirty pounds or less. Really fast runners were nonexistent. A 10.5 second hundred-yard-dash player was considered a speed merchant! In basketball a 6′ 0″ player was large and a 6′ 6″ player virtually unheard of.

IN COMPARING THE GAMES OF FOOTBALL AND BASKETBALL TODAY with the games fifty, sixty and seventy years ago we find today's players bigger and faster. The rules, the interpretation of the rules and the playing conditions are significantly different. The very nature of modern football and basketball is drastically different from the games of the first half of the twentieth century – a time of small towns and small schools, a time of high school coaches who truly were **COACHES FOR ALL SEASONS.**

Michigan-Wisconsin All-Conference players
from the Hurley Midget 1941 team:
Donald Harris, Dominic Moselle, Ted Thomas,
Joe Tomasin, William Zell

Coach Melvin, the "Wizard of the North Woods" (left)
and assistant, Teddy Gentile, the "Mighty Midget" (right),
1941

CHAPTER 3

THE GLORY YEARS BEGIN
1941-1942

FOOTBALL GOALPOSTS were not made to last. It was customary for a victorious visiting team to tear down the losing home team's goal posts. Because of this tradition, goal posts were usually two-by-four wood poles. The Ironwood Red Devils had dominated the football scene for so long that their fans boasted their goal posts would never be torn down. To protect their arrogance, they built the goal posts out of six-inch cast iron pipes sunk in concrete. They didn't expect to lose, but if the unbelievable happened their goal posts would still not come down.

Hurley's 1940 tie with Ironwood fanned the flames of their rivalry. Although this year's match-up with Ironwood was late in the season, from the beginning Coach's emphasis was Ironwood, Ironwood, Ironwood. Hurley hadn't beaten

Ironwood since the disputed game of 1920 and Hurley's fans tasted victory.

If you saw the two teams you might have had some doubts. Ironwood players were big - the biggest in their history. They averaged 190 pounds. The giant of them all was Matt Ulasch, the 240 pound butcher's boy from Jessiville (one of the small mining towns near Ironwood). He was so big and strong that in one game his kick-off went through the goal post's uprights for a field goal. The Red Devils outweighed the Midgets by thirty to forty pounds per man.

Three thousand fans packed Ironwood's Luther L. Wright Stadium for the Hurley--Ironwood Friday night game. I was ten years old and one of those fans. I'll never forget the scene, but I don't remember the game. I just remember, "We won!" The *Ironwood Daily Globe's* report of the game sums it up.

> Hurley had the better team last Friday night and as a result Hurley defeated Ironwood, 20 to 7. Only once during the entire game did Ironwood come within striking distance of Hurley and that was in the second period after Hurley had scored 13 points and Ironwood was trailing with seven points. Then and only then did it appear as if the weight advantage of Ironwood might wear down the courageous little Hurley Midgets. That was the only lapse Hurley had.
>
> It is no exaggeration to say that the Hurley team which rode victory on a T formation which was executed as faultlessly as the Chicago Bears execute it is one of the three best ball handling teams that has ever performed on the Gogebic range.
>
> Their Friday night game gave evidence they can rank along with the Leksell-Zambrovitz combination of 1926 and the Bessemer team of 1931 --two great aggregations. There is no question that the team is the finest Melvin has produced in

> Hurley.
>
> To coach Roy Melvin, grand chap if there ever was one, goes the credit for victory.
>
> Again we say—and we do not qualify the statement—that we believe this year's Hurley team is the finest team Melvin has ever produced and that the 1941 Lincoln high school aggregation ranks with the best the Range has ever seen. Give this team an average of 15 pounds more a man and it might defeat the average small college.

The Hurley newspaper, the *Montreal River Miner* reported:

> It was "Hurley Day" at the Luther L. Wright Field last Friday night. Coach Roy Melvin's Midgets put on the sweetest exhibition of football every seen around these parts as they administered a 20 to 7 defeat to the biggest Red Devil team in history. It was the first time that Hurley had defeated Ironwood since a disputed victory in 1920.
>
> Fans had heard that the Midgets were a smaller edition of the Chicago Bears. They were surprised that a high school team could master a modified T-formation....There are few teams in the country of the same size and weight that could have trimmed Hurley last Friday night.
>
> The well coached Midgets, pointed for this contest with their traditional rivals, functioned like a well oiled machine. They swept the Red Devils off their feet with their beautiful clicking formations, their accurate passing, their manipulation of laterals, and Hurley's forward line, although small in comparison with their opponents, never buckled.
>
> Year after year Melvin has pointed his charges for the game with Ironwood. Year after year he has had to swallow the bitter pill of defeat. He has proved that he is a bear for punishment, but being a good coach and a good sport, he has taken the spills with a smile, [all] the while hoping, always

> hoping, that a day would come that a win would turn up to warm the cockles of his heart.
>
> And this was the year. The '41 edition of the Midgets turned the trick.

When the final gun sounded bedlam broke loose. Michigan State Police were there for crowd control. The Iron County Highway Department, located in Hurley, was also there. They came equipped with acetylene torches. At the end of the game, they went out on the field and surrounded the goal posts. Some of the crew, with their blow torches turned on and facing out, held the Michigan State Police at bay as others cut down the goal posts.

Hurley fans rushed on the field. About a hundred Midget fans hoisted the cut pieces of Ironwood's cast iron goal posts on their shoulders; others lifted Coach and his assistant Teddy Gentile on their shoulders. Held high in the air, the goal posts and coaches led the parade of wild fans and honking cars as they traveled three abreast down the main street of Ironwood, across the bridge over the Montreal River, up Hurley's Silver Street to Fourth Avenue, heading toward Lincoln High School. On Fourth Avenue that sea of people and cars stopped in its tracks as it met up with Superintendent J. E. Murphy. The fans thought Mr. Murphy was going to stop the celebration. Instead he shouted, "Don't get me wrong, fellows, I just want to go under the goal post like the Hurley players did tonight. Ironwood is going to have to win it back!"

The pieces of the Red Devils' goal posts were displayed like trophies on the Lincoln High School lawn. On the following Monday morning Principal H. F. Connors called up the Iron County Highway Commissioner, Walter Williams, and asked him if he would be so kind as to use his equipment to return the goal posts to Ironwood. It just so happened that "Happy" Williams did not have any equipment. Hurley's souvenir hunting fans were busy with hack saws; Ironwood was busy getting new goal posts. The newspaper reporter from Ironwood described those Hurley fans:

> For 17 years we have wondered just how Hurley would act if they ever won over Ironwood. Last Friday night we saw the reaction.
>
> They acted as fine sportsmen. At various times we have commented on the fact in these columns that we have never heard Hurley boo an opposing aggregation. Friday gave evidence of how to act when you win.
>
> True, they celebrated last Friday night. Any town that would have scored the triumph Hurley did would also have celebrated. Yet Hurley didn't celebrate half as much as we imagine our town would have celebrated had we not defeated Hurley in a period that covers the life span of a new voter.

FOR ME, THE BIGGEST GAME OF THE YEAR, or for many years, was this win over Ironwood. On the Range, that year's biggest game was the Hurley-Bessemer game a week later – the game to determine the championship of the Michigan-Wisconsin Conference. It pitted young Coach Al Butherus and his heavy line that charged like a two-ton tractor with the Maestro Coach Melvin and his light brigade that played like a miniature Chicago Bears aggregate. If in 1923 you had told any football fan on the Range that in 1941 two undefeated teams would play for the championship, that neither team was the Ironwood Red Devils, and that both teams had beaten Ironwood earlier in the year, he would have thought you were hallucinating. But here they were—Hurley versus

Bessemer for the title.

Extra bleachers from Ironwood and Wakefield were brought to Bessemer's Massie Field, increasing the seating capacity to over 3,500. The seats were filled. With the standing crowd and those sitting in the upper seats of the adjacent baseball grandstand, the number of fans at the game was over 4,000. This crowd, larger than the populations of either Hurley or Bessemer, was probably the largest to see a high school football game on the Range.

Practically all Bessemer businesses closed for the afternoon. Mine workers went to work early that Saturday morning so they could get out in time to see the contest. Three bands, the two high school bands and the Bessemer township band, entertained the crowd.

The actual game was anti-climactic. It was over within the first two minutes. The headlines in the *Ironwood Daily Globe* read, **BESSEMER NEARS LEAGUE TITLE, BESSEMER LINE TOO MUCH FOR MIDGETS**. The opening paragraph of the article tells the story:

> The Bessemer Speed Boys virtually clinched the Michigan-Wisconsin Conference Football Championship Saturday afternoon at Massie Field when they capitalized on a break on the opening kick-off and pushed over a touchdown in the first two minutes of play to whip Hurley Midgets, 7 to 0 in a hard fought battle. ...The hero of the victory was Rudy Mikulick, Bessemer guard who fell on Bill Zell's fumble of the opening kick-off. A few plays later the brilliant Bill Velin scooted his own right end for twenty yards and a touchdown. The Hurley team lost some of its pep with that play although the Midgets made four marvelous goal line stands afterwards
>
> Bessemer was clearly the stronger team and the statistics bore that out — ten first downs to six,

> 220 total yards to 79. Although both teams were usually high scoring aggregates, this game was a defensive battle -- a valiant one considering that the Hurley team was battered, bruised, and tired from the epic battle with Ironwood. Harries and Erspamer went into the game as cripples. Moselle repeatedly tore into the Bessemer line and, on sheer power, made gains. In the last part of the fourth quarter the Speed Boys made four scoring threats and the Midgets made four successful goal line stands.

If this Hurley team was one of the three best to have played on the Range, you would have to add the 1941 Bessemer team to that group.

I FIRST BECAME AWARE of Dad's innovative coaching concepts in 1941. In this Bessemer game he installed a new method of defensive end play, designed to help control Bessemer's powerful running attack. Bessemer, like most teams in the North Woods, used the single wing offense. Standard defensive end play against a single wing was quite passive with both ends penetrating the line of scrimmage about three yards and then turning inward and waiting for offensive developments. Dad changed that. He had both ends aggressively crash in at sharp angles to attack the Bessemer blockers and ball carrier behind the line of scrimmage. Crashing into the lead blocker resulted in jamming the blockers before they could be fully deployed and occasionally knocking one blocker into another like a bowling ball hitting pins. This type of maneuver took the initiative away from the offense. It became the hallmark of Coach's future defensive strategies.

In 1939 Clark Shaughnessy of Stanford University introduced a new offense called the T-formation. The very next year the Chicago Bears hired Shaughnessy to implement the "T" for the Bears and it quickly became the talk of American football fans. Dad heard of it, but he never actually saw it played or talked to anyone who had seen it. He quickly saw its advantages for small, fast players, like his Hurley lads. Dad didn't just copy the "T"; he modified it.

In 1941, Coach introduced his modified "T" to his high school team and fans on the Range. It featured an unbalanced line and a quarterback facing the rest of the backfield. This reverse quarterback caused quite a stir among football fans. The newspapers called it Melvin's "butt-to-butt" formation. You can imagine what some of the fans called it. He put in the reverse quarterback to simplify the quarterback's footwork and facilitate ball handling between the quarterback and the other backs.

Dad's modified T-formation enjoyed immediate success at Hurley, producing a 6-1 win - loss record while amassing 203 total points. The "T" can't be credited for all of the team's success as the defense allowed only four touchdowns all season, never more than one to any team.

Dad's 1941 modified T-formation was by far the most significant innovation of his football coaching career. It started the long evolutionary process of Dad's offensive formation that eventually led to a single formation that incorporated the features of the known football formations: short punt (shot gun), double wing, single wing and standard T-formation. Not only was this an innovative feat but it gave his teams a big advantage.

LEGEND

QB = Quarterback HB = Halfback FB = Fullback TB = Tailback WB = Wingback X = Center o = Tackle = Lineman → = Back in motion

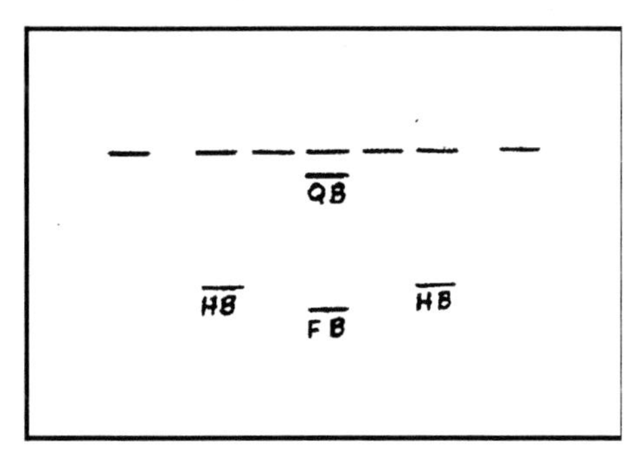

Diagram #1: Clark Shaughnessy's T-formation, 1939

The 1939 T-formation featured a balanced line and the quarterback under center facing the opponents. Either halfback could be in motion. This T-formation introduced a new blocking technique, sometimes referred to as "brush blocking."

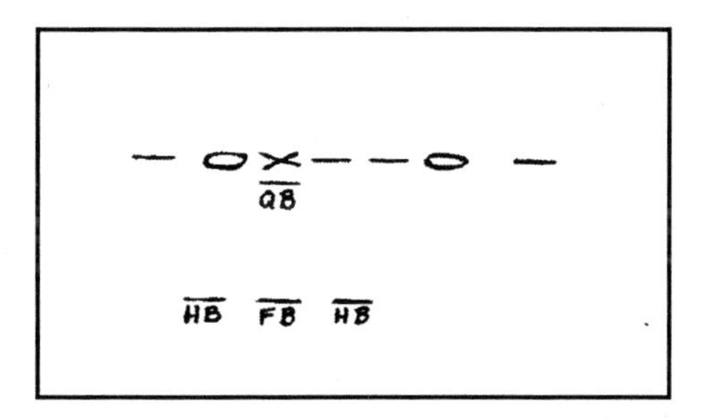

Diagram #2: Coach's Modified T-formation, 1941

Coach's 1941 modified "T" featured an unbalanced line right or left, a reverse quarterback under center facing his backfield. Either halfback could be in motion. This formation featured single wing and T-formation blocking techniques, passing from the quarterback and tailback position, and the full range of plays from the short punt, single wing, double wing and T-formation.

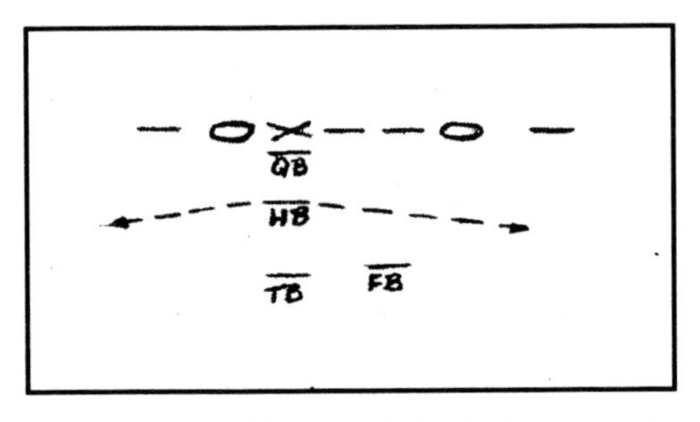

Diagram #3: Coach's Modified T-formation, 1944

Coach's 1944 modified "T" was a power formation, with the halfback in line with the quarterback and tailback.

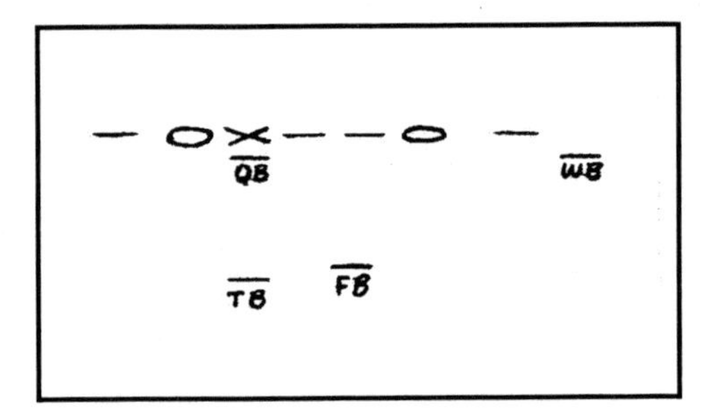

Diagram #4: Coach's Modified T-formation, 1948

Coach's 1948 modified "T" was a winged T-formation used to open up the passing game and reverse running plays.

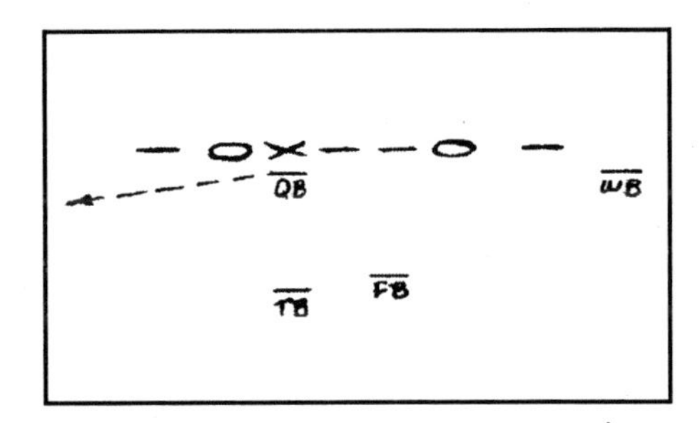

Diagram #5: Coach's Modified T-formation, 1950
Coach's 1950 modified "T" allowed for the full range of plays including double wing and spinning fullback series with the quarterback in motion. It also featured a direct snap to either tailback or fullback.

Diagrams 2-5 show the evolution of Coach's modified T-formation. In its final variation this single formation achieved the inclusion of the significant plays of all football formations: power sweeps, power cutbacks, spinning fullbacks, buck laterals, reverses, quick openers, pitch outs, draw plays, screen passes, shuffle passes, quick kicks and passing from either the quarterback or tailback position. Every known blocking technique could be utilized. Imagine the problems this formation presented the defense. For Coach, it allowed him to fit the system to his players.

Seeing Dad suited up in his red uniform on the field with his high school boys teaching them the modified "T" was quite a sight. Never one to be on the sidelines, Dad actually scrimmaged with his players. His distinctive red uniform cautioned his players that it was Coach they were hitting. The uniform wasn't foolproof. During this season he took a hit that broke his arm. At forty-four, the broken arm, "retired" Coach and his red uniform to the sidelines. On rare occasions he would come out of retirement and scrimmage. Even in his sixties he was a hands on coach, on the field demonstrating techniques or plays.

This season saw a first in Wisconsin football history. For some reason, unknown to me, Hurley played two games at the same time, on the same day, against two opponents miles apart. In his innovative way, Coach split the squad, taking Dominic Moselle with the second team to one game and sending assistant Coach Teddy Gentile with the first team (minus Moselle) to the other game. Hurley won both games.

ON DECEMBER 8, 1941 the newspaper headlines screamed: **JAPS BOMB PEARL HARBOR**. Life in America changed for everyone, especially for the millions of young men and women who entered military service. Dad, a naval veteran of World War I, volunteered for service with the U.S. Navy. He was offered a commission as Lt. Commander and assigned to train enlistees at a base in Alabama. He turned down the commission because, as he said, "If I'm going to be in training, I might just as well stay at Hurley and prepare the boys for military service." We were staying in Hurley!

Hurley's Lincoln High School, circa 1935

Ashland High School – Main building

CHAPTER 4

BALANCE OF POWER SHIFTS
1942-1943

COACH WAS STARTING HIS TWENTIETH YEAR in Hurley. He had seen a lot of players come and go from Lincoln High School since his first Hurley team took to the field. Back in 1923, his current assistant coach, Teddy Gentile, wasn't even in kindergarten, county supervisor, Paul Santini, who had given fans thrills on both the high school gridiron and the court, was only in third grade and Lenny Calligaro, Hurley's own gridiron hero on the University of Wisconsin 1942 football team, was still in diapers. Coach, considered by many the dean of Range coaches, looked back and reminisced, "I haven't had many great players all on one team, but I sure have had some honeys in my day."

And then those days were over! Folks on the Range were stunned when they opened the August 21, 1942 *Montreal*

River Miner. The headlines announced: **MELVIN RESIGNS HURLEY POST TO TAKE SIMILAR POSITION AT ASHLAND.** What they read was almost unbelievable!

> Coach Roy E. Melvin of Hurley High School, better known as Mel to his many friends and just about an institution at Lincoln High, resigned his post yesterday after 19 years to accept a similar position at the Ashland High School, starting September 1.
>
> The Midget mentor is one of the most popular coaches the range has known and many friends who will be sad to hear he is leaving Hurley will be glad to know that he is staying in the Michigan-Wisconsin conference and that his teams will continue to play on the gymnasiums floors and football fields of Ironwood, Bessemer, Wakefield and Hurley.
>
> Baseball is the sport that brought Melvin to the Range a couple of decades ago. He came here to play with the Hurley team, managed to make the grade where many others had failed and remained to become a legend at the Hurley High School.
>
> Supt. J. E. Murphy, who met with the school board last night to consider Melvin's resignation, said today that no decision has been made as to who will succeed Coach Melvin
>
> 'It's going to be mighty hard to replace a coach like Melvin,' Mr. Murphy remarked. 'We had come to consider him almost as an institution at Hurley High School.'

The Hurley fans couldn't believe that Roy Melvin had decided to go somewhere else. In his "Sports Comment" Armand Cirilli expressed the mood in town:

> For almost 20 years Orange and Black athletics has been synonymous with the talkative Melvin. Now he's gone and he will coach the Ashland teams.... It will be hard to get accustomed to seeing another

> man working with the Hurley athletes. It will be even more difficult to believe that in a few weeks Roy Melvin will be on the other side of the field conniving and planning against Dom Moselle and company. This winter fans will have to acclimate themselves to viewing fingernail-biting Mel on the enemy side of the gymnasium he has waited and prayed for. It's a funny picture. But it's true.

We were leaving Hurley! I couldn't believe what Dad had done. Why? Just a few months earlier, when the Japanese bombed Pearl Harbor and we entered World War II, Dad considered leaving Hurley for the war, but didn't. Dad had been in Hurley for nineteen years and the fall before had bought our first house. You don't buy a house if you're going to move. Dad had the total support of the school administration and the community. They were building his dream – a big new gym. This was the year he'd get to play in it. He finally had an assistant, his own Teddy Gentile. His family was crazy about Hurley.

I couldn't understand it then and, sixty years later, I still can't. Two answers came from Dad himself. Days after Dad resigned, the *Ironwood Daily Globe* printed a picture of Dad with the headlines **ROY MELVIN SINGS SWAN SONG.** It was Dad's farewell to Hurley. He said, "No one will know how much I wanted to stay in Hurley this year, but the offer and opportunities at Ashland are much too good to turn down."

Was Ashland a better offer, one too good to turn down? Maybe Ashland offered more money. But I've never known anyone less influenced by money than Roy Melvin. Was there more athletic talent at Ashland? Dad had great talent returning this year in Hurley. He always said that Don Dick in basketball and Dominic Moselle in football were the best players he ever coached in those sports and both would be back for their senior year. True, Ashland was a bigger city—almost three times bigger than Hurley -- but, it had two high schools. If Ashland hadn't had two high schools, the talent pool at Ashland High would certainly have been greater. But with the high school population divided, Ashland High's enrollment was only slightly larger than Hurley High's.

Dad's other answer as to why he left Hurley came many years later. "I guess I got ambitious too late in life."

Ambitious? Dad had lots of offers. He had standing offers to join the coaching staffs of Harry Stuhldreher, head football coach at the University of Wisconsin and from Steve Owens, head football coach with the New York Giants. Over the next ten years Dad would receive numerous coaching offers from high schools and universities. Bo McMillan, head football coach at Indiana University spent two days at our home trying to convince Dad to join him at Indiana University. Dad would turn them all down. That doesn't sound like an ambitious man.

IT WAS A STRANGE AUGUST. One day Coach was in Ashland handing out purple and gold jerseys to his new Ashland High School squad. He was out on the practice field drilling them in fundamentals, emphasizing conditioning. A week later he was back in Hurley helping Assistant Coach Gentile pass out the black and orange uniforms to his former team, giving "his boys" one last pep talk.

As fate would have it, Coach's opening football game pitted the Ashland Purgolders against the Hurley Midgets and the incomparable Dominic "Jabs" Moselle. I remember asking Dad, "What are you going to do about Jabs?"

That question was to be asked by a lot of teams that fall, but Dad would have the first crack at the answer. He responded, "We'll box him in."

The scheduled Friday night game was changed to the following Monday because the Ashland field was a sea of water and mud. That didn't stop a deluge of Hurley fans from driving the thirty-eight miles on a Monday night to see this match-up.

The game was played under ideal conditions. Coach had, by now, started utilizing the concepts that later became known as his "shooting the gap" defense. He employed these techniques using both defensive ends to box-in Moselle. The defense was well conceived and repeatedly trapped Moselle behind the line of scrimmage for big losses. I can still see him ...Moselle receives a hand-off...starts in one direction... is cut off...turns and goes the other way...all the time giving up ground...trapped again...zigzagging back and forth. At the end of the third quarter the game was tied 6 to 6. The newspaper account of the fourth quarter tells the rest of the story:

> Moselle was almost thrown for about a seven yard loss, but amazingly he got away and when he was finally stopped he had made a first down. The next play is the one that dazed the Ashland team, fans and even the Hurley coach. Mrdjanovich tossed a pass to Moselle who ran a bit before he appeared to be tackled. Then he threw a lateral to Thomas who also looked like he was stopped who in turn tossed the ball to Bottacin, who came out of nowhere, for a touchdown. A few plays later Ashland again got into a hole on a poor kick and shortly after Moselle again sailed over for a touchdown.

Although thoroughly outplayed, Hurley won 18 – 6. That night Moselle proved to me his football greatness. Not only was he a great runner, he was just as good on defense. He was also a terrific punter, the best I've seen other than a few professional punters. Although losing, the Ashland fans sensed the makings of a winning team, a team that outplayed a tough Hurley team.

The fans were right. Coach brought a winning 4 – 2 record to the final game of the season. Despite the winning record, Ashland was considered a big underdog against league-leading Bessemer. The 1942 Bessemer Speed Boys were on their way to repeating last year's unbeaten season record and the Michigan-Wisconsin conference title. No one gave Ashland a chance. Coach devised a special defense utilizing defensive end blitzes. On a windy, snowy Saturday night in Bessemer, the fighting Purgolders pulled out a stunning upset, winning 14 – 7. After the Bessemer game the *Ashland Daily Press,* in talking about how Coach had given Ashland fans something to be proud of, said: "Coach Melvin has worked wonders in the eight short weeks he has been at the helm."

He gave Hurley fans something to be proud of too. When the Michigan-Wisconsin Conference was formed in the 1930s, Dad had publicly predicted that Hurley would win a conference football championship by his twentieth year of coaching. This was his twentieth year. He was no longer the coach of Hurley. But his Ashland win over Bessemer meant Hurley shared the conference title with Bessemer. On the trip back to Ashland, Coach had the school bus driver go into Hurley and stop on Silver Street. He hopped off the bus, went into one of the establishments and announced, "I delivered on my promise." The Ironwood newspaper gave a lot of press to that Ashland game, ending with "The fantastic part of this tale is that Roy Melvin couldn't give Hurley a title while he was their coach, but he played a major part in giving them a share of it from his post at Ashland."

Looking back, I think Ashland's victory over Bessemer was one of Dad's biggest wins. Years later one of his players on this victorious Ashland team, Paul Tomlinson said, "He took over football and basketball teams with losing records and completely changed the win - loss columns with practically the same players." The football team finished 5 – 2 and the basketball team 15 – 4, including two wins over the great Hurley team.

ONE THING CAN BE STATED WITH CERTAINTY about Dad's move to Ashland. For sports on the Range the balance of power in the Michigan-Wisconsin Conference shifted from Michigan to Wisconsin. In football, Hurley's 1941 victory over Ironwood and Ashland's 1942 win over Bessemer signaled the crumbling of the Ironwood and Bessemer sports' dominance of the '20s and '30s. It forecast the emerging dynasty of Hurley and Ashland in the '40s. The strong athletic tradition that Dad built at Hurley continued through the 1940s with coaches Carl Vergamini and Mario Giannunzio. In the regional tournament Hurley beat good Ashland and Superior Central teams to advance to the Spooner sectional. Because of the war there were four, instead of the usual eight, statewide sectional meets. This meant an unusually tough sectional roster. Hurley and a powerful Chippewa Falls team dueled for the sectional championship. The Chippewa Falls' team starred Nate DeLong, a 6'8" high scoring center. Few could stop him from scoring twenty or more points a game. Hurley's Don Dick guarded DeLong in that championship game. At the end of the first half the score was Hurley 24, Chippewa Falls 1! Hurley won 41 – 25. Coaches, Vergamini and Gentile, and their Hurley Midgets were heading to Madison for their first state basketball finals. Armand Cirilli in his weekly sports column in the *Montreal River Miner* thought another coach should also be there:

> We would like to see Roy Melvin go to Madison to see the Midgets play there. After all he carried these boys along for three years. He was so happy when they defeated Superior Central although he had to be neutral. The Hurley boys like Mel and no doubt he could give them lots of encouragement and even some advice in Madison.

Roy Melvin took Armand Cirilli's advice and was in Camp Randall Field House for "his boys" when they lost the opening game to the eventual state champions, Racine Park. Hurley went on to finish third in the state tournament – a stunning finish for a school with an enrollment of approximately three hundred fifty students. Clark Van Gilder, the coach of the Racine Park champs, told Dad that he believed Hurley would have won its game if Dad had been on the Hurley bench, and eventually would have become state champions.

Hurley's Don Dick was high point scorer in the twenty-sixth state basketball tournament finals. What is unusual about that record is that Dick was not known for high scores. Quiet and smart, Don Dick, at 6′ 0″ and 170 pounds, was a master of the fast break, a terrific passer who got the ball to his teammates and a great shooter who only shot when others couldn't. He was one of those unselfish players who made all his teammates better. It was his defensive skills, as "Red" Nylon, "Bud" Grant, Jim Lucas, Nate DeLong and others can attest to, that complete the picture of a great player.

A NUMBER OF FACTORS CONTRIBUTED TO THE SHIFT OF POWER in the Michigan-Wisconsin Conference. First and foremost was the change in Michigan eligibility rules. By the 1940s rough parity in Michigan-Wisconsin eligibility rules was achieved. Until this parity was achieved Wisconsin teams couldn't successfully compete against Michigan schools.

Other factors contributed to this shift: Dad's move to Ashland, resulting in strong athletic programs in both Wisconsin schools, the elimination of the center jump rule and the building of new modern gymnasiums in Ashland and Hurley. By the mid-1940s Hurley and Ashland teams dominated the Michigan-Wisconsin Conference.

"The Recruits"
Chuck Yderstad, Dick Axness and Keith Carlson

CHAPTER 5

EYE TO THE FUTURE
1943-1944

WHEN DAD MOVED TO ASHLAND he said it would take three years to establish his program. The 1942-43 season had been a good start. He had two years to prove his soothsaying talents. His skills were well suited to achieve his prediction. Although he didn't know the difference between a hammer and pliers, he was a builder; although he had never worked in sales, he was a walking public relations man; although he wasn't a professional talent scout, he had an eye for athletic ability.

1943-44 was a rebuilding year for both Hurley and Ashland. In Hurley, Coach Carl Vergamini left for military service and Mario Giannunzio took over as coach. In Ashland, Dad began to build a year round athletic program. He knew the program would pay dividends in athletic success in future years. Besides football and basketball, he increased participation in track and introduced tennis. In a few years Ashland High School dominated tennis in the Michigan-Wisconsin Conference. Dad was in charge of the summer recreation program, which included playground activities at the three grade schools, swimming at the east and west end beaches, and tennis, basketball and softball at the high school. At Dodd Gym, badminton, ping pong, volleyball and basketball were available.

Dad had a strong belief that getting less experienced players into the action was an important role of sports. The *Ashland Daily Press* quotes him as saying:

> I find throughout the ages that in the leading nations the youth predominated in games. In the days of the Spartans and Athenians, where running was the chief activity, the youth were healthy and vigorous.
>
> As soon as professionalism came into being the youth deteriorated—that is, the youth who were not expert enough to participate in certain activities would quit sports, and thereby get soft.
>
> It is a good thing to have new players take over the jobs of those who leave the team. The players fight to make first team—if the same team held over we would have a school of sitters.
>
> There is a continuous turnover. The boys are all competing, with an incentive of playing instead of observing.

From Dad's earliest days in Hurley his actions bore out this philosophy. In one game with a half time football score of 39 to 0 in favor of Hurley, he turned the team over to his assistant and reserves and took several of the regular players to scout the remainder of a Bessemer-Wakefield game. In another year and another game, he actually used three separate teams for one basketball game. Just before the close of the first half he sent in his entire second team. Four minutes into the third quarter, the third team went in. At the start of the fourth quarter the first team took the floor back. These combined "three teams" won 20 – 12.

Throughout his career at Hurley and Ashland he continued to use reserve players whenever possible. This was not a common practice among coaches of that era. For Dad, it accomplished two important goals: inexperienced players got valuable playing time and scores didn't get too high against weaker opponents.

This year, with his "green" football and basketball squads, Coach emphasized conditioning and fundamentals and giving all players playing time. In the regional basketball finals, Ashland's 29 - 27 loss to the strong Superior Central team was a sign of things to come.

No one could have predicted the "things to come" resulting from Coach's eye for talent and his ability to convince boys to participate in athletics.

In the spring of 1944 Ashland hosted the district basketball tournament for the small schools. I went to some of the games with Dad. Sitting with Dad in the bleachers, I heard him make a startling comment, "Dick Axness is going to be one of the greatest players I'll ever have at Ashland."

I had never heard him make predictions about individual players in high school so I began to concentrate on Axness and his play. What I saw was a tall, gangly player who seemed uncoordinated and quite awkward. I scoffed. "That kid is going to be one of the greatest basketball players you will coach in Ashland?"

"Yup!" was his quick reply.

I was totally puzzled. The kid was on the Mason High School basketball team. Dad never recruited a player from another school. He explained to me that he didn't have to recruit him because Mason was a two-year high school and Axness would have his choice of Ashland or Drummond high schools for his junior and senior years.

"But how do you know he'll choose Ashland High School?"

"I'm going to talk to his parents." Dad did. He didn't talk about the educational advantages of Ashland High over Drummond, but rather Dick's chances of getting financial assistance from a university because of his basketball talents which would be better displayed at Ashland High. The next year Dick Axness was seen on Ashland's gridiron and basketball court.

That August Dad and I were driving past the high school when he stopped the car and pointed out the window. "Do you see that boy walking up the steps of the high school? He's going to be a top football player."

I saw this husky kid that I'd never seen before. "Who is he?"

"Charlie Yderstad".

I'd never heard that name and I knew all the football players by name. I thought Dad was crazy. "He's not even out for football!"

Dad's reply was simple. "No, but he will be."

"How do you know he'll be a good football player?

"He's tough, smart and determined!"

Well, he did look tough, and Dad was a teacher so maybe he knew that he was smart, but determined? "How do you figure he's so determined?"

He grinned and told me the story about Charlie and his

buddy Keith Carlson. How they once spent eighteen hours digging fox cubs out of a den. I remember thinking. "Maybe that is determination, but was it smart?" Charlie justified Dad's assessment. He became one of the best football players to play for Ashland High School.

Years later, during my fiftieth high school class reunion, I ran into Keith Carlson, Charlie Yderstad's buddy in the fox digging incident. While talking about Dad, Keith said that Coach had tried to talk him into playing football, but it conflicted with his fall trapping activities, so he wasn't interested in playing. Playing in spring was another story. Keith showed up for track that next spring. He became the premier distance runner in northern Wisconsin.

So, before the 1944-1945 season began, Coach had successfully convinced new players to wear the purple and gold. These three - Dick Axness, Charles Yderstad and Keith Carlson—became three of the best athletes to play at Ashland High School in the 1940s.

Dad didn't limit his perceptive and persuasive powers to individuals. He did a great deal of public speaking and woven into his speeches were frequent appeals for community support for youth. Excerpts of these "community sermons," such as the following challenge to the Presbyterian-Congregational Church's Men's Club, were often recorded in the press. In stressing the need for a backlog of funds for youth, the *Ashland Daily Press* quotes Coach:

> Instead of cutting taxes when times are good, communities would be far-sighted to put away a sum for that purpose [youth].
>
> The first and fundamental thing for a boy is to burn up energy. Give them something built around games. A ping-pong table is fine, but generally it

> is a meeting place where the youth make plans to go somewhere else. If we would combat juvenile delinquency we must keep the youngster busy – physically.
>
> Arts, crafts and music are fine, but that isn't enough for the youth. He'll run into trouble unless he burns up energy. If we could get young men working with our fifth graders, our worries would be over.... We should begin training the boys from the fifth grade. There would be no smoking, swearing and other bad habits that we see today.

SOME FOLKS THOUGHT ANOTHER KIND OF RECRUITING brought Coach to Ashland. Since 1933 the public Ashland High and the Catholic DePadua High sponsored an annual two game basketball series. The rivalry was so fierce that some people thought Coach was brought to town to beat DePadua.

For the fans, these two games were the biggest games of the year. They drew the biggest crowds – so big that they were called the "Pack'em In" Series. In 1932 Ashland and DePadua played a one game fundraiser to raise money to send DePadua to Chicago to play in the National Catholic High School Tournament. It was a successful fundraiser. It was even more successful as a crowd pleaser. The following year, two games were scheduled and a new Ashland tradition was born.

The early games were played in DePadua's small gym and DePadua never lost a game. In 1937 Ashland High School had a new modern gymnasium, Dodd Gym ... the talk of the North Woods. The "Pack'em In" Series moved to Dodd Gym. The new gym had a huge entrance foyer on the north end, a stage on the south end, bleachers on both east and west sides, and large floor areas at both ends.

The crowds at these annual two clashes filled the gym and stood six deep under the baskets. The stage, normally occupied by the band, was converted to seats for the fans. Usually rabid fans packed the foyer just to be there listening to the game on the radio and hearing the wild hoopla of the live crowd. The newspaper warned fans to be there when the doors opened at 6:00 p.m., be seated by 6:30 for the 8:00pm game or they'd be part of the standing room only crowd. Sometimes the players experienced the crowd up close and personal. I remember having to push the crowd back in order to get my feet out-of-bounds so I could throw an inbound pass. After the ball was out of my hands a DePadua fan held my pants to prevent me from getting back in the action. I stomped on his toes and he let go of my pants.

When Dad arrived in Ashland, the series stood DePadua twelve wins and Ashland eight. In his very first season his team won both games against DePadua and started reversing the losing trend. In his nine years coaching at Ashland, Ashland High School monopolized the series, winning all but one game, bringing the series total wins to Ashland twenty-five and DePadua thirteen.

ANOTHER KIND OF RECRUITING WAS GOING ON in all the nation's high schools. Each year thousands of boys graduated from high school and enlisted or were drafted into military service. Each year some still in high school traded in their basketball and football uniforms for army green. At seventeen a boy could enlist in the military and some did. More chose to enlist in the second semester of their senior year as this gave them their choice of military branch. The draft at eighteen tore many others away.

The war and its effects absorbed everyone's psychological

energies. There was a chilling starkness to the newspaper's daily front page box listing local war casualties. There was a collective sadness to the gold stars appearing in windows: stars signaling a son lost and a community's future diminished. Life would never be the same for anyone!

The 1943 Ashland High School yearbook, the Wawata, declared "Our peace time Wawata has gone to war."

The Ashland High School 1944-1945 Basketball team
Front row: Bob Howard, Bob Hanson, Ken Tidstrom, Vern Fryklund, Myron Bystrom, Harvey Johnson–Back Row: Coach Melvin, Bruce Fossum, C. Nelson, Dick Axness, Les Howard, Duane Ruth, George Papadakis

CHAPTER 6

TALE OF TWO SEASONS
1944-1945

"NOT SO BAD ... NOT THE BEST, BUT NOT BAD" was the prediction around town about the winning prospects of the 1944-45 basketball team. Bruce Fossum was the only returning starter from the previous year's team. "Skyscrapers," Les Howard, George Papadakis, and Duane Ruth as well as speedy Jake Konkol were back. Then there was the new kid Dick Axness. They were a tall bunch; they were a promising, but unproven, bunch!

A sold out crowd at Dodd Gym got its first glimpse of the 1944-1945 Ashland team with Ruth at center, Konkol and Howard at forward and Fossum and Papadakis at guard. The team started slowly and then pulled away to defeat a young Hurley team 29 --23.

Three days later, Ashland traveled one hundred miles to Rhinelander for a close, hard fought game against the

Rhinelander Hodags. Ashland won 29 – 26, but lost its sparkplug, Jake Konkol. After the game he caught a midnight bus to Milwaukee and joined the Army.

The first game without Jake Konkol was at Superior East on November 28. The tall junior transfer, Dick Axness, replaced Konkol at forward, giving Ashland the distinction, unusual for that era, of having five starting players all over six feet. By the end of the first quarter the Purgolders had an 11 to 3 lead. At the end of the game, with nine of ten players seeing action, they easily won 29 – 15, having allowed a good East team only five field goals.

Ashland barely won its fourth game. Although the Purgolders led all the way in that December 8 game against the Bessemer Speed Boys, they were lucky to win 26 – 24.

The December 15 game against Harry Conley's powerful Superior Central Vikings would indicate the strength of this Ashland team. Both teams had won their first four games, with Central scoring over forty points per game. The incomparable Harry "Bud" Grant led Central's all-veteran team. Grant was ably supported by second year starters Don Bredahl, Tommy Ward, and Ken Polglase, as well as transfer Jim Hoppenyan. At this point in the season, Central was the best team in northern Wisconsin and probably the best in the state. Central not only matched Ashland in size but also had considerably more experience. Central had home court advantage; Ashland was a decided underdog.

The Ashland five utilized a man-to-man defense. Their uniform size and defensive skills were well suited for this type of defense. Coach assigned Bruce Fossum to guard Bud Grant. The game plan was to slow Grant down, make him work for every point and box him out from offensive rebounds. There was no thought of stopping him cold. He was simply too good. This strategy worked and Grant scored fourteen points on five field goals and four free throws, considerably below his twenty-five points per game average. The game was tied repeatedly, seesawed back and forth, and was played with only one substitution. With seconds to go, the score was tied at 28 to 28. At the final gun Bruce Fossum made a long set shot. The underdogs won 30 – 28. What a win! A great gift for Coach on his forty-eighth birthday!

The very next day, after the big win over the Vikings, the Purgolders beat John McDonald's undefeated Park Falls Cardinals on their under-sized court. Every member of the traveling squad saw action and contributed to the 42 – 28 victory.

Ashland ushered in 1945 with a 6 – 0 record and a maturing starting five. Dick Axness was beginning to demonstrate his scoring skills. The team's defense and rebounding were awesome. The first game of the new year was against Wakefield. Headlines in the *Ashland Daily Press* after that January 5 game blared: **ASHLAND HIGH SCHOOL LANDS ON WAKEFIELD**. Ashland defeated Wakefield 57 – 22 with Dick Axness scoring twenty-two points. To quote Bruce Fossum:

> Once Axness started to 'feel his oats' so to speak, Coach put in a weak side screen for him which popped him open near the free throw line for his patented one-hander or good head fake and drive to the basket. Dick's one-hander was the closest thing to a jump shot that I ever saw. He wasn't given credit for inventing it but he probably should have been.

On January 10, Coach Bill Knoblauch's undefeated

DePadua Bruins arrived at Dodd Gym hoping to defeat Ashland for the first time since Coach's arrival in 1942. The DePadua team, well matched against the bigger Ashland five, was expected to give Ashland a tough battle. The standing room only crowd experienced another easy 42 – 24 win by the Purgolders. The opening paragraph of the account of the game tells it all:

> Displaying an airtight defense that held their opponents to five field goals, the Ashland High School basketball team won its eighth straight game of the season and the first of the two game series for the city championship by defeating a scrappy but outclassed DePadua team 42 to 24.

Dick Axness led all scorers with twelve points. Coach used all twelve players in the victory.

In a slow, poorly played offensive game at Hurley on January 12, Ashland won 29 – 16. They allowed Hurley only six field goals. This Ashland squad was developing into an overpowering defensive team. Fossum, Howard, and Papadakis were terrific defensive players; Axness and Ruth were better than average. At the beginning of the season George "Pappy" Papadakis had boasted that he wouldn't shave his mustache until Ashland lost. Seeing Pappy around town sporting his mustache reminded everyone of a winning team. Mid-season and undefeated!

On January 19, Ashland won its tenth game, easily defeating the Bessemer Speed Boys 45 – 26. In this runaway game both teams sent their subs in to play the entire fourth quarter. As one Ashland sportswriter observed, "You know, it's just dawning on a lot of people that Ashland has one of the best basketball teams in the history of the school." It was a bit early to crown the team "the best." Ashland still had to face second games with Superior Central, Park Falls and DePadua and two games with a very good Ironwood team.

Coach cleared the bench again in an easy 31 – 18 win against Superior East on January 20. Les Howard, the big 6'3" forward, led all scorers with ten points and, more importantly, was emerging as a complete player.

The headlines for the year's final Ashland versus DePadua game read: **FINAL GAME OF THE "PACK 'EM IN" SERIES.** DePadua came into this game with an 8 – 3 record versus Ashland's 11 – 0. DePadua was led by Jim Pentony, the top scorer of either team. Surrounded by Bob Molaski, Don Miller, Tom Casey and younger brother Jack, they made a fine quintet. DePadua scored nine field goals. They held Ashland to only six field goals. In this very close match, free throws made the difference. Ashland's 25 – 21 win was a very close call.

Jake Konkol, home on furlough, traveled with the team to Wakefield to watch all twelve of his former teammates see action in Ashland's 40 – 27 rout.

Five days later, when Park Falls came to Ashland, it was a different story. At the end of the half Park Falls led 14 to 8. In the third quarter Ashland scored twenty-two points; Park Falls scored five. Coach turned the game over to the second "five" for the last quarter. Ashland won 45 – 25, allowing only seven field goals in the entire game. Coach had worked his half time magic!

With Ashland's 14 - 0 record, Ironwood's coach, Jack Kraemer, knew what he was up against, and he was getting ready. Ashland fans joked that someone should find out if Kraemer was living here because he's here for every game. This first match-up between Ashland and Ironwood promised to be another great game between two undefeated teams. It was! Ashland won 38 – 27. In the "Highlights and Sidelights" section of the *Ashland Daily Press*, Kelly and Kelly, Jr. wrote:

> Well, it's fifteen down and two to go now for the Purgolders to have a perfect season. But those two to go are going to be tough ones and make no mistake about that – Superior Central here next Friday night and the Red Devils at Ironwood a week later.

Now, on the road to a perfect season, came the game of the year – the rematch with the tough Superior Central Vikings! Ashland came into the game 15 – 0. Superior Central had a 15 – 1 record, its only loss to Ashland. Fans came from all over northern Wisconsin to see this game. Dad told me he had a surprise waiting for the Vikings. "I'm going to turn Dick Axness loose tonight." He did! Axness scored twenty of Ashland's thirty-eight points and Ashland won easily 38 – 26. Bruce Fossum held Bud Grant, Superior Central's great forward, to ten points. The Ashland defense allowed only ten field goals. The starting five played the entire game. They dominated all phases of the game. They crushed Central. Ashland jumped to number two in the statewide basketball rankings. Superior Central fell to twelfth.

This team had matured. It was on the verge of a perfect season. With one game to go Coach sensed that, after the great win against Superior Central, the team was getting overly confident, maybe even a bit cocky. They were, after all, just seventeen-year-old kids. That week after a bad practice, Coach told his players to run laps and then shower. Captain Bruce Fossum skipped the laps and went right to the locker room to shower. The manager came in and shouted, "Bruce, Coach wants to see you!"

When Fossum arrived in Coach's office, Coach quietly said, "Bruce, run your laps." Bruce vividly remembers going down to the locker room, putting on his basketball gear, going up to the gym and running, running, running. He didn't stop until he couldn't run any more. Then he said to himself, "Lesson learned!"

The last game of the regular season pitted the undefeated Ashland Purgolders against the Ironwood Red Devils, a team with only one loss, that at the hands of Ashland. The Purgolders were on the crest of a wave of wins. Sports writers joked that Pappy would be an old man before he shaved his mustache. Could they complete a perfect season? Played in Ironwood, this last game of the regular season was a toss-up. At the end of the first half Ironwood led 17 to 16.

Coach put on one of the most dramatic half time performances of his long coaching career. The players filed into the locker room and quietly sat around. Coach didn't show up. I was astounded. Where was he? His team needed him. The conference championship and an undefeated season were at stake. Was he sick? What had happened? Time passed. The quiet got louder! With about two minutes remaining of the half time, Coach entered the locker room, and walked around the room looking each starting player in the eye. Then he said, "Do you want to play your way and lose or my way and win?" Almost in unison the players responded, "Your way, Coach!"

There was a knock on the door and the referee announced one minute to game time. Coach requested an additional minute and got it. He then explained to each of his starting five players precisely what they were to do in the second half.

In that second half Ironwood scored only seven points. The final score was 40 – 25. Ashland had won! Everyone talked about the offensive surge Ashland put on in the second half. I was in that locker room at half time. Coach only gave defensive and rebounding instructions!

What a year! Ashland High School had an undefeated basketball season for the first time in its history. They had their first Michigan-Wisconsin conference championship. They had a tremendous team nearing the height of its prowess, a great team with no stars, or all stars, depending on how you looked at it, a terrific defensive and rebounding unit. It was a great season!

GAMES	FINAL SCORE	WINNING MARGINS
Ashland vs Hurley (H)	29-23	06
Ashland vs Rhinelander (*)	29-26	03
Ashland vs Superior East (*)	29-15	14
Ashland vs Bessemer (H)	26-24	02
Ashland vs Superior Central (*)	30-28	02
Ashland vs Park Falls (*)	42-28	14
Ashland vs Wakefield (H)	57-22	35
Ashland vs DePadua (*)	42-24	18
Ashland vs Hurley (*)	29-14	15
Ashland vs Bessemer (*)	45-26	19
Ashland vs Superior East (H)	31-18	13
Ashland vs DePadua (H)	25-21	04
Ashland vs Wakefield (*)	31-18	13
Ashland vs Park Falls (H)	45-25	20
Ashland vs. Ironwood (H)	38-27	11
Ashland vs Superior Central (H)	38-26	12
Ashland vs Ironwood (*)	40-25	15

(H) = Home games (*) = Away games

THE SECOND SEASON, THE SUDDEN DEATH BASKETBALL TOURNAMENT, was about to start. Ashland would be there; the Superior Central Vikings would be there too! As Kelly and Kelly, Jr. said in the *Ashland Daily Press*:

> Very prominent among the spectators at the game [Ashland versus Ironwood] was Harry Conley, Superior Central coach, whose team is almost sure to tangle with the Purgolders again in the regional tournament here [at Ashland] next week. If any local players or fans have an idea that Conley has given up hopes of beating Ashland in the tournament, just stop and figure out why he made a little trip of about 230 miles to see Ashland play [Ironwood] last night.

There was no quit in Harry Conley or his players. The WIAA ranked Ashland number two and Superior Central number nine. Now, the real ranking would begin.

There was a strong field of contenders in the 1945 Ashland Regional Tournament. Four of the eight teams had outstanding records: Ashland at 17 – 0, Superior Central at 15 – 2, Park Falls at 13 – 3 and Philips at 13 – 4. The two powerhouse teams were Ashland and Superior Central. Some experienced observers thought that these two high school teams were the best ever to play in the upper Mississippi River Valley.

The Thursday night opening games matched Ashland with Phillips and Hurley with Superior Central. Everyone expected Ashland and Superior Central to win easily and go on to face each other on Friday night. They also predicted that the winner of that game would win the regional and the sectional championships to advance to the state finals in Madison. Many also thought that the Friday night winner would be the eventual state champion. But tournaments are won by playing, not voting.

Ashland beat Phillips without much trouble, winning 42 — 23. Superior Central had plenty of trouble with Hurley, finally winning 32 — 27. Expectations became reality. The third game of the tournament featured a third game of the year between Ashland and Superior Central. Coach was really concerned. Beating any good team three times in one year is tough, and Superior Central was more than good—it was great. Coach, opting for no change in the game strategy, used a man-to-man defense, with Bruce Fossum on Bud Grant. It was another epic battle. The game was won in the last seconds with a shot by Papadakis. Ashland won 30 — 28.

In the regional championship Ashland beat Park Falls for the third time that year, 43 — 28. Park Falls' season was over - a season in which it had lost only four games, three of them to Ashland. As regional champs, Ashland would be traveling to Spooner for the sectional tournament.

The Monday before the sectional tournament the *Ashland Daily Press* headlines told a shocking story: **HOWARD LOST TO BASKETBALL TEAM**. Les Howard had enlisted in the U.S. Navy with the understanding that he wouldn't report for duty until after the State Basketball Finals in Madison. But bureaucracy is bureaucracy! Les Howard received his orders to report and he was lost to the team.

The four teams in the Spooner sectional were Ashland, Drummond, Spooner and Cameron. Ashland drew Drummond, a very good team led by Newman Benson, one of the best passing and shooting guards ever to play in northern Wisconsin. Even without Les Howard, Ashland won 45 — 7. Spooner beat Cameron in the other game. In the championship game, Ashland beat Spooner on their home court, 61- 24. In both sectional games, Ashland's reserves played most of the second half. It appeared that Ashland had weathered the loss of Les Howard. The Purgolders, the only undefeated team in the state, moved on to Madison for the eight team state finals.

It was one thing to win a relatively weak sectional tournament without Les Howard, but the state finals would be tougher. The 1945 State Basketball Tournament final roster was:

TOURNAMENT TEAMS' SEASON RECORDS	WINS	LOSSES
Ashland	22	0
Madison West	19	1
Lena	23	1
Tomah	20	1
Wisconsin Rapids	19	1
Waukesha	19	3
Eau Claire	15	4
Berlin	13	7

Madison West ranked number one in the state; Ashland ranked number two; Wisconsin Rapids, Tomah and little Lena each had only one loss; Waukesha was the returning state champion. When Ashland opened play on Thursday against the number one ranked Madison West team, they quickly found out how tough the field was.

Predictions favored the team winning the Ashland-Madison West match-up as the final state champion. Henry J. McCormick, writing in the *Madison State Journal* said:

> There are some things about this 30th annual WIAA

> basketball tournament which I think can be stated definitely. One thing of which I am reasonably certain is that the crowd at Thursday night's game is going to come very, very close to being the largest in the history of tournament play in Wisconsin. The big reason for that, of course, is the fact that the powerful aggregation representing Madison West and Ashland will tangle in a first round game that may very well decide the ultimate.

Well, McCormick was right. The winner was the ultimate state champion. McCormick continued:

> Another thing of which I am convinced is the fact that the tournament field this year is strong. Coach Roy Melvin of Ashland regards Madison [West] as the biggest stumbling block between his lads and a state championship, and he admits he is worried more over that first game Thursday night than he will over any foe he may meet Friday or Saturday.

Coach was concerned about Madison West. They were ranked number one for good reason. They had an outstanding team led by center Don Paige and guard Bob Smith. Playing in one of the toughest leagues in the state, they had only one loss. Coach had never seen them play. Who would replace Les Howard? None of the reserves could match Les' talent, size or experience. He would be missed, especially on defense. There was no time to make adjustments. It was game time!

Fossum held Don Paige to one field goal and six points. Papadakis held Bob Smith to one bucket and one free throw. But West's John Wise scored seventeen points! Madison West led all the way, winning 34 — 26. Bruce Fossum said it best:

> No one knows better than I how much we missed Les Howard at the [Wisconsin] state tournament.

> He seemed to always be around the basket and knew how to get open. Some good chemistry was missing. The other kids tried hard to fill his shoes but the talent was just not there.

The dream was over! On Friday night a clean shaven Pappy and his teammates defeated Tomah 22 – 17 and, on Saturday night, lost to Waukesha, 15 – 14, to finish fourth in the state. Madison West beat Eau Claire, 52 – 34, to advance to the finals against Lena. Little Lena, with a town population of approximately 500, was the fan favorite. In the end, Lena fell to Madison West's superior size and depth. West won 44 – 35 to become the 1945 Wisconsin state basketball champions.

No one was more disappointed than Coach. He didn't get to coach his great Hurley team in 1943 and it lost to the eventual state champion. Now he had lost two of his regulars to military service and lost the opening game to the eventual state champ. The Ashland team could afford the loss of Jake Konkol, but not the loss of Les Howard. They needed Les' rebounding and defensive skills. The perfect season was over. The final record wasn't perfect, but the team was close to perfect. This was the best high school basketball team I have ever seen.

After the tournament, thinking about how we missed Les Howard, I sometimes wished that we hadn't defeated Superior Central and that they had gone on to the state. Maybe with their team intact they would have represented the North with a win!

Years later I mentally speculated how this Ashland team would have fared against Dolph Stanley's great 1945 Taylorville, Illinois High School team. What a classic match-up that would have been: a great offense against a great defense. Fifty-five years later Captain Bruce Fossum reminisced about his team:

> To sum this team up: we all [the regulars] had talent and good size. We ran a very simple offense and actually ran a lot, though the scores in those days don't show it. We ran a lot in practice and our condition was impeccable. That, besides Coach's defensive teaching, made us tough to score on. He was the master; the catalyst that made our engine run. I worshipped the guy!

Fortunately, Coach did not believe that "winning is everything"! To Les Howard, Jake Konkol and the dozens of others from Hurley and Ashland high schools, he hadn't lost. He had helped prepare them for the bigger game of life.

THE BIG NEWS IN THE LIFE OF THE NATION was the end of the war. In May we celebrated V-E Day, victory in Europe, and in August V-J Day, victory over Japan. Almost sixty years later I can still feel the electricity in the air. The war was over! The boys were coming home!

Coach and the starting five of the
"Team That Could!"

Clockwise: Coach Melvin, Bob Howard, Bob Hanson,
Dick Axness, Clyde Carter, and Keith Hinds.

CHAPTER 7

THE TEAM THAT COULD
1945-1946

THE MASON YOUTH WITH MAGNETIC MITTS, Dick Axness, arrived in Ashland as a junior in the fall of 1944. In his junior year he lettered in football, basketball and track. By this, his senior year, he had matured physically, from that awkward boy I had seen eighteen months earlier, to a well coordinated 6'4", 190 pound athlete.

The football team, with four starters from last year, Axness, Fred Tidstrom, Charlie Yderstad and Marvin Hunt, played solid football. The season ended with a 5-1-1 record, marred only by a heartbreaking 9 — 6 loss to Ironwood. It seemed that Ironwood would always be our nemesis.

The real story of 1945-46 was BASKETBALL! Many thought this would be a rebuilding year after losing four of the starting five from last year's dream team. Coach departed from his usual concept, moved Axness to center and built a team around a single player. As the season progressed the inexperienced players matured and by tournament time Ashland had a very good team.

Dick was a perfect student: smart, hardworking and, more importantly, willing to learn. Coach took advantage of this and taught Dick a new shot each week. Dick worked on that shot all week. As the season progressed it was more and more difficult to defend him. Teams resorted to two-teaming, and in some case, three-teaming him. Even that couldn't slow his record setting scoring pace.

By the middle of the season this Ashland team ranked thirteenth in the state. It was a good team, but certainly not a great team. The same could not be said of Axness. He was a great player and the greatest scorer in the history of Wisconsin high school basketball. His season high 407 points in seventeen games broke Johnny Kotz's record of 403. His single game fifty-four points scored in thirty-two minutes of play was an unbelievable record.

Axness' individual game and season point tally were always big news in the sports coverage of the Purgolders' games. Such publicity could have been hard on the other players, but Coach publicly praised his team. "I have a team of kids without jealousy. If any jealousy had cropped up we wouldn't have had a team." Built around a star, the team became progressively better and better. The team wrapped up the season with a solid 11 — 6 record.

The big four of the North Woods in the 1940s, Superior Central, Superior East, Hurley and Ashland, went head-to-head at the regional tournament at Hurley. The two Superior teams were clear favorites, having beaten Ashland twice and each other once. Opening night fans thrilled to two hard fought contests. Ashland nudged Superior East, 24 – 22; Superior Central edged out Hurley, 28 – 26. The next night Hurley nosed out Superior East by one point for a 24 – 23 victory and Ashland stunned Superior Central with a 29 – 27 victory. This tournament was another example of the tough competition the four schools provided in the regional tournament. In the four games, a total of only seven points separated the winners from the losers.

Ashland welcomed home their "tired" champs. These boys had taken a lot of punishment. Three tough games in three consecutive nights! Two nights without much sleep! The first night they had to spend a few hours in the hotel lobby because there was a small, smoky fire in their hotel. The second night, they were kept awake by the rambunctious, door-pounding boys from the eliminated teams. Exhausted and exhilarated, the team that "proved they could" arrived home to prepare for the sectional tournament.

That week during a Kiwanis Club talk, Coach paid a glowing tribute to the spirit of this team. After acknowledging the tremendous play of Axness, especially his rebounding, he pointed out the contribution the others made. In particular, he commended their defensive effort in holding Superior Central scoreless for nineteen and a half minutes in the 29 – 27 win. He ended his talk with these words. "We adopted a plan and all of the boys fell in with it and gave it their best."

What was "the plan" that Coach referred to in his speech? The plan was a zone defense. Yes, a zone! In the twenty-eight years at Hurley and Ashland I know of no other season when Coach utilized a zone defense. His mind and philosophy were against it. But his team had lost by big scores to the two Superior schools and Coach knew that they would, no doubt, play one or both at the regional tournament.

The zone defense was particularly effective against a bigger team or a hard-driving team. It placed and kept the five defensive players inside the offensive players, giving them rebounding position. It was not so good against a fast break, a good moving and passing team or a good outside shooting team. Superior Central and East were big teams, not prone to fast breaks and not particularly good at outside shooting. Every year Coach worked one or two weeks on a 1-2-2 zone. Other than this year he never used it. Coach continued to use this zone defense throughout the remainder of the state tournament.

After tough regional battles, Ashland ran away with the sectional championship title, with easy wins against the Rice Lake Warriors and the Clayton Bears. In the 58 – 41 championship victory over the Clayton Bears, the Purgolders scored forty-three points in the second half. Axness broke the existing tournament record of thirty-one points per game with a new forty-one point record: a high that could have been higher if Coach had not taken Dick out.

With the sectional tournament behind them, the team, packed into three cars, left Ashland for the state finals, stopped in Marshfield for lunch, in Wisconsin Rapids for a short practice and arrived in Madison for tournament play.

Ashland's first game of the tournament was a duel between two centers - Ashland's Axness and Eau Claire's Hoff. Axness won the scoring duel with seventeen points to Hoff's ten points. Eau Claire won the game, 38 – 33. On Friday the Purgolders roared back with a close 29 – 28 victory over Beaver Dam and advanced to the consolation game. The largest high school tournament crowd watched Ashland and Racine Park battle for the consolation title. Outside the rain poured. Inside, the field house roof leaked in three places and the boys were slipping on the wet hardwood floor. At one point the game had to be stopped so the referee could escort a dog off the floor. Racine Park took an early lead and led for most of the game. Even though Ashland's defense prevented Racine Park from scoring a field goal from late in the third quarter to the final horn, and. Dick Axness was top scorer with twenty-four points, when the final buzzer sounded Racine Park was the consolation winner.

Dick Axness came into the tournament the highest scoring state prep player with a twenty-four point average. He left Madison as the tournament high scorer with a total of sixty-three points in the three games, one point less than the all time scoring record set by Rhinelander's Johnny Kotz in 1939. Ashland returned home with a 17 – 8 season record, finishing fourth in the state.

THE BIGGEST TOURNAMENT SURPRISE was another North Woods' team. Reedsville, with a total student body of eighty-seven, defeated Eau Claire (population 46,000) whose 1,600 student body was more than twice the size of Reedsville's total population. That win crowned Reedsville the 1946 Wisconsin State Basketball Champions!

Coach and Stu, 1932

CHAPTER 8

A DAD CALLED COACH
1946-1950

I WAS DADDY'S BOY and the Coach's kid. Mother told me that by the time I was a toddler I could sense when it was time for Dad to get home from school. I'd press my nose against the front window pane and repeat over and over. "Daddy come ... Daddy come ... home." When I was in grade school, I didn't go home after school like the other kids. I went up to the high school to hang out with the "big guys." I knew all the players and I was like a kid brother, sometimes cute, sometimes a pest, but always there. Once a new player, a senior transfer, who wasn't used to my running underfoot in the old Hurley gym just picked me up and stuffed me between a locker top and the ceiling. I was stuck there until another player rescued me. By the time I was in seventh or eighth grade I was old enough to go on the team bus to some out of town games.

My little brother and sister never rode on the team bus, but there was no doubt that they were the Coach's kids. Summer mornings Maggie and Tom and the neighborhood kids hitched a ride with Dad to Sandbar Beach in Ashland. Dad, as head of the city's recreation program, made morning and afternoon trips to both city beaches to check on the life guards, and the neighborhood kids rode along. In the fall Mom filled the car with Tom, Maggie and the cheerleaders for the trek to Hurley for the Hurley-Ashland football game. Tom learned every cheer, knew all the cheerleaders and, at home games, sat right behind them ... their unofficial mascot. Maggie napped on the cheerleaders laps and felt they all were her big sisters. We all had kid-size tennis rackets almost before we had bikes, and those wonderful leather bags filled with shinning marbles from the city marble tournament. In the dead of winter, we'd practice our marble shooting on the living room carpet. The circular flower designs were perfect for marble games. Long before there were family rooms with pool tables, the ping pong net was a permanent part of our dining room table, and the cause of a lot of arguments. It was oval, so great corner killer shots were a disaster. I can still see Maggie drawing the imaginary corner with her hands and arguing with Tom that her corner shot should count because it would have been good if the table had a corner.

Although we all grew up as the Coach's kids, I was the only one who actually played for Dad. My first coach was Bill Knoblauch, my eighth grade coach at St. Agnes Catholic School; my last coach was Pill Nelson, at Beloit College; in between I played for Dad, called "Coach."

I always knew that I would play for Dad. For Mom and Dad it was a little more complicated. Dad wasn't Catholic;

Mom was. When they married Dad had promised to raise the children Catholic. In the immigrant church of the 1940s raising children Catholic meant sending them to Catholic schools. My parents had to get permission for me to attend the public high school. That was probably made a little easier since Dad was a tennis partner with Father Francis, the parish priest, and permission was probably granted over the tennis net.

After all the years of shadowing my Dad, all the years of playing pickup games in the neighborhood, and my one year playing on a real team, I dreamed of playing football, basketball and tennis ... for my Dad. What I didn't know was that, seeing Dad in action, not just in the games, but behind the scenes, I would start to understand the way he thought about sports and life. By the end of those four years, I realized that I had played for a great coach. I cherish that experience.

THE SUMMER OF '46 WAS UNUSUAL. The boys who had gone off to war were coming home. I remember a steady stream of Hurley and Ashland players, just home from the war, stopping at our house to see Dad...every week...all summer long. One local lad, Howie DeBriyn, a big man who had been a senior on Dad's first team in Ashland back in 1942, just wanted to go fishing with Dad that first summer back from combat. He and Dad went fishing on the Kegonsa Sloughs at the mouth of the Bad River. On one of those trips Dad invited me to go along. We fished all day and caught lots of walleyes. I was quiet, waiting for Dad and Howie to talk about sports and the war. There was hardly any talk – just two men and a kid fishing. Dad later said that those boys had seen and done things no one should ever have to experience. They needed time to heal.

Hurley's Jabs Moselle was home from the war and all set to play for Coach Fritz Crisler at the University of Michigan. But that fall Jabs was playing at Superior State Teacher's College. When I asked Dad what happened to the University of Michigan, he simply said, "Jabs just isn't ready to play in the big time. He just needs time to adjust without too much pressure."

"How'd he get to Superior State?"

His answer was simple. "I called Ted Whereatt at Superior State." Jabs played four years at Superior State. Later he went on to play with the Cleveland Browns, the Philadelphia Eagles and the Calgary Rough Riders.

Years later I commented that Jabs playing at Superior State had made Michigan's "Bump" Elliot an All-American. Dad laughed and said, "Probably!" I also began to realize that Dad was a second father to many of his players, a father who listened and intuitively understood.

AUGUST CAME with its hint of the north's early fall. Dad asked me, "Are you going to play football in the fall?"

I had already learned that when he asked a leading question or an obviously ridiculous one, I had a problem. I carefully answered, "Yes!"

His second question revealed my problem. "What are you going to do with your paper route?"

I hadn't thought about that, but the answer was obvious. "I'll deliver papers after football practice."

I saw his head shake; I heard his "no" almost before he opened his mouth. "Your customers expect their papers delivered between four and five in the afternoon. You'll have to decide what is more important, your paper route or football!" In a few days I sold my route for $5.00, the profit I made in one week. Dad was a genius at picking the right moment to teach a lesson, whether in sports or life. This was one of the more important lessons in my life: You sometimes have to make hard choices.

By far the biggest lesson I learned from Dad wasn't a lesson, but a strategy. Whenever I was faced with a perplexing situation, I asked the question, "What would Dad do?" and I had the answer.

My paper route was gone; the summer was over; I entered Ashland High School. For the next four years I called my Dad "Coach" at school and "Dad" at home.

LIKE ALL OF HIS PEERS, Dad was a teacher first and foremost. As a teacher he always put the kids first. Dad believed that the sport was for the players, not the coach or the fans, and that it should be fun for the players. He had strong relations with his players, even the opponents' players. In my junior year during a football game with Hurley, two big tough Hurley players, Carl Hermanson and Eugene Martino, ran into each other, were knocked out and ended up overnight in the Ashland General Hospital. After the game, Dad went to the hospital to visit the injured players. When Carl saw Dad the first words out of his mouth were, "How's Stu?" I guess Hurley's goal had been to get me out of the game. But Dad wasn't there about me. He was there to visit the two Hurley players. I think Dad still considered them his boys.

As a coach for all seasons Dad was involved with many sports and players over the course of a year. In some cases his coaching involved individuals who didn't play on any of his teams.

In the early 1980s I ran into an old Ashland friend, Dale

Moore, who invited me to have a drink. When we got our drink he began to tell me what an important influence Dad had on his early life. I had heard theses stories from others, but always from former players. Dale had never played for Dad so his comment piqued my interest.

It seems that Dale approached Dad in a physical education class and asked him to teach him how to box. Dad agreed and took time from the remainder of the school year to teach Dale to box. These lessons had obviously impacted Dale's life.

DAD DESIGNED HIS SYSTEM to fit the available player talent. He didn't fit the players to his system. He was the architect of the plays; his players executed them. In both football and basketball, he used the locker room for team instructions or psychological ploys. In football he gave specific instructions to individual players while he was taping them or with them on the field during pre-game warm-up activities. In basketball he was actually on the court with his players during pre-game and half time warm-ups. He moved among the players, talking to them individually and giving assignments. Because he almost always utilized a man-to-man defense these individual assignments were critical to his strategies.

My first personal introduction to these assignment talks occurred when I was a sophomore. I hadn't played during the first half so I was surprised during the half time warm-up of the Superior East game when Coach took me by the elbow and said I would be starting. He told me I was to guard Hennessey. Hennessey wasn't to get a set shot or to drive to his right (my left). His next instructions amazed me, but I was in no position to challenge him. He said that I was to overplay Hennessey to my left, so that my legs straddled his right leg, and that I was to get up so close to him that he couldn't shoot his favorite set shot. Hennessey was a very aggressive player and I was to make him run over me. The second half started with me, a skinny 130 pound kid right in Hennessey's face so that he couldn't shoot. He got a bit frustrated and thought he could run over me. Hennessey repeatedly fouled. I repeatedly shot free throws.

Hennessey didn't score a point the second half and I learned a big athletic lesson. This basketball lesson had broad implications: never doubt Coach's instructions! He may have lost his wits as a Dad, but he certainly knew what he was about when coaching. There would be many other assignment talks in the next two and a half years, but none more impressive to me.

BY THE MID-1940S, BASKETBALL RIVALED FOOTBALL as the king of sports in the North Woods. There were a number of reasons basketball became popular. The elimination of the center jump rule changed basketball from a slow game to a fast exciting game. The building of new modern gymnasiums with full size playing courts and large seating capacities encouraged large crowds. The long hard winters, lasting a good six months, drove most activities indoors. Basketball was a perfect indoor activity.

Dad's reputation was that of an innovative football coach, but those of us who played football and basketball for him knew that he was just as creative in basketball. It just wasn't as apparent. There were no revolutionary offensive formations, no dramatic new defenses, no reverse quarterbacks, and no "shooting the gap" linebackers. Dad's basketball teams looked much like other teams. The differences lay in subtleties and tactical concepts.

Dad started each basketball season with the same short speech to his assembled squad. He would detail what he expected from the players, the team as a whole, and the practice routines, all the time tossing the ball in the air with one hand. I heard this speech four times, consciously missing the real message. With no words, he was telling us, "This is what we play with, **the ball - get it, keep it, guard it**!"

Physical conditioning was the cornerstone of his teams and running was at the heart of his conditioning program. Not every player or team necessarily had basketball talent but they would be in excellent physical condition. They wouldn't lose the game in the fourth quarter because they "ran out of gas." All of his football and basketball practices ended in running. If the practice was unsatisfactory it might end in "duck walking." Once you duck walked around a football field in full pads you didn't have many bad practice sessions. He was helped in his conditioning program by the fact that virtually all of his basketball players played football in the fall and either tennis or track in the spring

Dad often combined conditioning with other aspects of coaching. For instance, each discipline infraction incurred a running penalty. If the penalty was suspension the offender was offered the chance to work off the suspension by running after practice for a week or two. This gave the offender a face saving alternative, improved conditioning and discouraged others from breaking rules.

In basketball he ended practice by having a free throw shooting contest. The losers ran laps and the winners showered. This tended to improve team free throw shooting and conditioning. A variation of this contest was Coach against the entire team. If any member of the team beat him,

Coach ran laps and the team went to the showers. If Coach won, all members of the team ran laps. Coach never lost this contest.

COACH BELEIEVED DEFENSE WON BASKETBALL GAMES and that every player, regardless of his talent, could be a good defensive player.

There were three elements to Coach's defense: the player must be in excellent physical condition, he must be determined to stop his opponent, and he had always to be in the correct position relative to the basket, the ball and his opponent. This defensive concept resulted in the player being in the best position when his opponent received the ball.

Defense was the hallmark of his basketball coaching. I never heard him swear, but he had one four letter word heard by all players: "move"... "move" ... "MOVE"!

Coach's defense was unique. It actually began when we had the ball. It ended by getting a defensive rebound and transitioning to offense by looking for a fast break opportunity. His half court offense, which varied depending on the talent of his players, always featured a "back guard."

The back guard concept had one player, usually a guard, remaining in the back court. His job was both offensive and defensive. In the event that the offensive play was unsuccessful, the back guard would receive an outlet pass and a new play would be started. If the opponent got the ball, the back guard was to stop that opponent from advancing the ball. He did this by forcing the ball to be picked up and preventing the fast break from developing. This gave the other four players time to "get back on defense." During my years of playing for Dad, we never gave up a fast break score.

Most of Dad's peers in the North Woods coached a similar style of half court offensive basketball and man-to-man defense. The differences in Dad's approach were in assignment (match-ups) and adjustments. This was his genius. His match-up and adjustments were so logical and simple that I never thought anything about them, until it dawned on me that the other coaches saw the same things he did, but didn't make those little adjustments.

Maybe that is why Dad shunned the use of film in sports. I don't think he ever looked at a film of his own team or any of his opponents. He once told me that the worst thing to happen to football coaching was the film. With the advent of film most coaches never learned to analyze what was happening in real time, when they could still make adjustments in the game. He disdained the delayed response that film allowed. I think of him today when I hear professional coaches in their post game responses to a question about a play, say "I can't comment until I've reviewed the film." It's almost like the coach wasn't there to see the play.

DAD WAS A MASTER AT PSYCHOLOGY. I'll never forget my senior year, especially the Monday of the week preceding the 1949 Hurley — Ashland football game. Dad began a psychological ploy to prepare us. We heard "Hurley this, Hurley that," until we had Hurley coming out of our ears. There was no special defense. We scrimmaged day after day. We listened to his incessant talk of Hurley. We were all sick of Hurley ... and him.

The game was played on a beautiful fall night. It was made more beautiful when we beat Hurley 19 - 0. We dominated the game, offensively and defensively. Without any special defense or plays we completely outplayed the Hurley team. Apparently Coach's psychological ploy was effective, especially considering the season ending records: Ashland ended with a 3 – 5 record. Hurley ended with a 7 – 1 record, a record which included a season ending victory over the powerful Superior Central.

In my junior year I experienced how Dad tailored the game strategy to the situation. It was a late season game played against Superior East, under the night lights of Superior State Teachers College's barren football field. At game time the weather was bad and getting worse. Rain threatened. A strong wind was sweeping across the field.

We won the toss and chose to receive. Defending the south goal line, we had the wind at our back. With rain drops already in the air, Coach predicted the weather would deteriorate and any scoring would happen early in the game. He took me aside and instructed me to receive the kick-off, return it a few yards and punt the ball over the heads of the onrushing East players. I kicked the back half of the ball so that it would tumble on the bare ground and then watched it roll like tumbleweed until it stopped on East's six yard line. East failed to get a first down and had to punt into that strong wind, giving us the ball on East's thirty yard line. We fired two quick, unsuccessful passes. On third down Larry Lindholm, making a circus catch, scooped the ball from the top of his shoes and bowled over a defender to score a touchdown. We converted the extra point and led 7 to 0.

Coach was right again. The weather worsened; the rains came; we played ankle deep in mud. The game deteriorated into a punting match. When either team got the ball, they ran to the sidelines to get dry footing and punted the ball.

Our team punted at least twenty times in those forty-eight minutes. Superior East scored a touchdown in the fourth quarter but, with the mud and the wind, couldn't convert the extra point. That "mud bowl" game ended in our 7 – 6 win. It also ended our uniforms. They were so soaked with mud that we had to throw them away.

COACH ALWAYS HAD A SET OF TRICK FOOTBALL PLAYS. One of the funniest plays was his peanut play. I don't know why he called it the peanut play. He probably got the idea from the early days when there were no hash marks. Without hash marks, the position of the dead ball determined the ball's position for the next play. When the ball was dead close to one or the other sidelines, all offensive linemen had to line up on one side of the center for the next play. With the advent of hash marks, these line-ups virtually disappeared, but not in Dad's mind. I think this was the genesis of his peanut play where all the linemen lined up left or right of the center. All backs went to the strong side. The quarterback lined up behind the center. The right alignment looked like this:

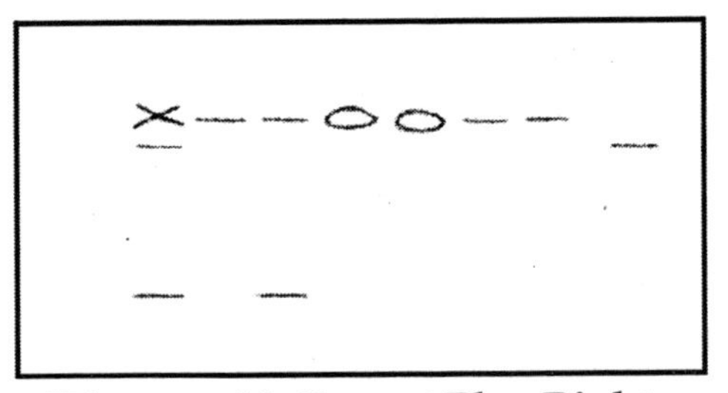

Diagram #6--Peanut Play Right

Because the center was on the end of the line, he was an eligible pass receiver. After touching the quarterback's hands with the ball, he could keep the ball and run.

This was the peanut play. We practiced it every season, but I only remember using it once. During our homecoming game against Superior Central in my junior year, we had the ball on Central's three yard line with first and goal. In three downs we failed to score a touchdown. On fourth down, Coach called for the peanut play right. We broke the huddle and lined up six linemen to the right of center. The Central team was totally confused. I can still see their players running around in disarray. We snapped the ball. Our center, now the left end, kept the ball and stepped into the end zone for a touchdown. He could have run a hundred yards untouched. The peanut play was good for one touchdown and added a little spark to this homecoming game. Superior Central was still the better team. They won 20 — 7.

HAVING A FEW TRICK PLAYS MAY BE INNOVATIVE, but it was unheard of to initiate a whole new offense in mid-season. That's exactly what Coach did one season at the end of our fourth game. We had lost three out of four games. We had scored a total of only five touchdowns. We had no offensive punch. Coach scrapped our offense and installed a standard T-formation with a few wrinkles. Coach's new T-formation featured an unbalanced eight man line with the quarterback under center and two set backs. It also featured hiking back (into the backfield) any one of the six linemen. This feature caused considerable confusion to the defense and provided unusual blocking patterns and angles. Defenses started to wait until the lineman hiked back. Then when we didn't hike back we would catch the defense napping. In the 1980s when the Chicago Bears pulled "Refrigerator" Perry and put him in as a running back it was the talk of the football world, as if it were a big deal. Dad had been doing that way back in the

'40s. His schemes, however, were a lot more innovative. In his system he could hike back any one of six players who could then block, receive a pass or carry the ball.

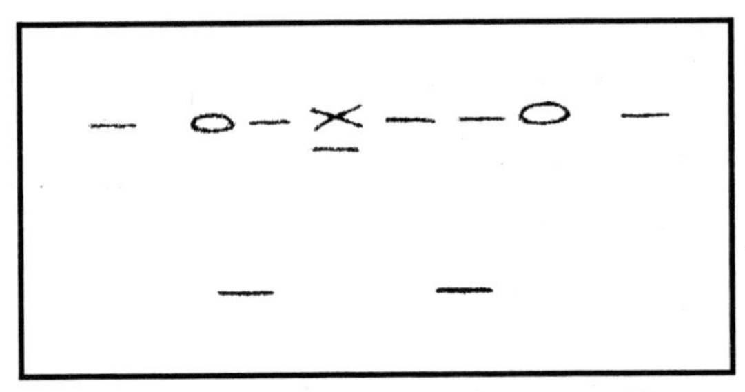

Diagram #7 – Eight Man Line Offense

The formation was successful. We won three of our last four games. In these three wins, Ashland's team scored seven touchdowns.

I NEVER SAW DAD'S PLAYBOOK. When I asked him where he kept his plays, he just looked at me and pointed to his head. One of the reasons he didn't have a play book was that he didn't need one.. His modified T-formation had evolved to the point where he had incorporated all four of the popular football formations into a single formation with standard nomenclature, alignment and blocking. With this all inclusive formation he could add a play or series of plays with minimal change and practically no teaching. For example, if he wanted to add a spinning fullback series of plays to his double wingback formation, an unheard of concept, all he had to do was change the play designation. All blocking and backfield maneuvers except for the quarterback were the same. This single formation concept also facilitated his philosophy of fitting the system to the player.

THERE WERE ONLY A FEW TIMES WHEN BEING THE COACH'S SON affected me. In my sophomore year I was slated to be on the basketball starting five. Prior to the first game, I started to sense a bit of resentment on the part of some of the team's upper classmen. After all, I was only a sophomore, and, I was the coach's son. I couldn't handle the situation. I quit the team. This was the most difficult time of my young life. I had looked forward to playing high school ball and it looked like it was all over. Dad and I didn't talk about my quitting and that made the situation even worse. For him it must have been hell. For me, I anguished and did heavy workouts each day after school. I grew up a lot during those couple of months and was in the best shape of my young life.

I couldn't stand not playing. After Christmas I rejoined the team. Although I wasn't a starter, I was the sixth man and I saw plenty of action. I didn't have any problems with my teammates and I didn't have any problems with Dad as my coach. I did have the usual teenage problems with parents. My parents got dumber and dumber as I got smarter and smarter. Magically they recovered their wits by the time I graduated from high school. An amazing process!

CARRYING GOOD LUCK CHARMS was common among coaches. Dad's was a scruffy old rabbit's foot. For every game or contest it was in his pocket. As far back as I can remember he had this rabbit's foot. Then one year it disappeared. Dad and mother turned the house upside down; no rabbit's foot was found. A disaster! I didn't believe in lucky charms and the lost rabbit's foot proved my disbelief. Dad lost his lucky rabbit's foot during the 1944-45 perfect season.

IF I HADN'T BEEN THE COACH'S SON, I never would have played baseball. Up until 1948 no northern high schools had baseball teams. The WIAA prohibited interscholastic competition when school wasn't in session. The North's weather severely hampered any spring sports. Despite that, Coach did have spring track and tennis programs. I remember shoveling snow off the tennis courts and wearing gloves while playing. In a climate that seemed to go from winter to summer and simply miss spring, a baseball season with a full conference schedule was impossible to fit in before the end of school year. Spring was just too wet, cold and short. It didn't get warm and dry out until the ice left Lake Superior and that could be as late as June 1.

In 1948 the WIAA finally recognized the weather problems in northern Wisconsin and permitted high schools in the north to play baseball in the summer. The Michigan-Wisconsin Conference teams and Park Falls immediately began baseball competition.

Because the northern football season started in early August, the baseball season was still short, so two games per week were scheduled. This required a minimum of two pitchers. Dad had only one. He had to develop another pitcher in a hurry so he decided to recruit me to pitch.

I liked contact sports. I wasn't all that fond of baseball. I had never pitched. So, when Dad asked me to help him out, I argued a bit, but I finally agreed. We didn't have much of a team, but we tried. I was known as Ashland High School's strike-out king, but the wrong kind of strike outs. I struck out frequently as a batter!

During a baseball game at Ironwood, we were at bat when I spotted this enormous, broad-shouldered guy walking across the infield toward our dugout and the thought "that's Tom Kirby" drifted through my head. Sure enough it was. He had come to offer Dad a job at Warren (Michigan) High School. He was president of the Warren School Board and, it seems, he had convinced the Board of Education that his high school coach was the one to coach Warren High School. Dad turned the job down, but I got to meet "five yard" Kirby.

Dad loved baseball. It was what brought him to northern Wisconsin. Although I didn't really enjoy baseball, I was glad to help Dad get baseball started at Ashland High School.

THE SUMMER I TURNED FOURTEEN I was ready to play my first football season for my Dad, the Coach. I could see myself in that purple and gold uniform. As the start of the school year approached, I wondered if there would be a season. Rumors were flying that the start of school might be delayed due to a polio outbreak. Some northern school districts did delay the start of the school year. What I couldn't possibly know, as I thought about my first football season, was that the polio scare would give us our greatest game.

WAUSAU DAILY RECORD-HERALD, WAUSAU, WISCONSIN

PAGE TWENTY-ONE

WAUSAU HIGH SCHOOL

FOOTBALL SEASON

OPENS SAT., SEPT. 10

with a

"Booster Game"

with

ASHLAND HIGH SCHOOL

Get behind the team this first game and follow through the entire season with your attendance and enthusiasm. A "Brechmeyer-coached-team" means the best in high school football and you'll want to see whether your school can maintain its unbroken string of victories. See every game!

HOME SCHEDULE

Saturday, Sept. 10, Ashland
Booster Day

Saturday, Sept. 17, Marshfield

Friday, Sept. 30, Antigo
Homecoming

Saturday, Oct. 22, Wis. Rapids
Dads' Day

Season Tickets Still Available

AT PLOSS DRUG COMPANY

4 HOME GAMES $3.40

Including Tax

Reserved Seats for Single Games, 85c

GENERAL ADMISSION

Adults, 74c—College Students, 50c

High School and Grade Students, 25c

OUT OF TOWN SCHEDULE

Friday, Sept. 23, St. Point
at Stevens Point

Saturday, Oct. 8, Rhinelander
at Rhinelander

Friday, Oct. 14, Eau Claire
at Eau Claire

Saturday, Oct. 29, Merrill
at Merrill

This Space Is Contributed By The Wausau Advertising Pool—Devoted to Community Interests and National Welfare

Full page announcement from the *Wausau Daily Record Herald* (09/1949)

CHAPTER 9

DAVID VERSUS GOLIATH
1946 and 1949

IN FOOTBALL CERTAIN GAMES TAKE ON A LIFE OF THEIR OWN: the 1946 Notre Dame versus Army game, the 1958 NFL championship game between the Baltimore Colts and the New York Giants, and the 1966 NFL Championship "Ice Bowl" game between the Green Bay Packers and the Dallas Cowboys, to name a few. In Wisconsin high school football, the 1946 Ashland High School versus Wausau High School contest was that kind of game.

To many people in the United States the name Wausau conjures the image of a railroad station with the sign "Wausau" from Employers Mutual of Wausau's national TV advertisement. To Wisconsin high school football fans, Wausau is the story of high school football dominance spanning the period from the late 1930s to the mid-1950s. There were other outstanding football programs in the state but none compared to Wausau

High School, the premier football school. Playing in the strong Wisconsin Valley Conference, Wausau High School lost only one football game from 1937 to the early 1950s, a span of over one hundred games. In 1946 Wausau boasted a forty-six game winning streak. Even more stunning was their record of sixty-nine straight games won or tied in a ten year period, a record reputed, at that time, to be the longest undefeated streak in United States high school football history.

Wausau High School was coached by Win Brockmeyer, a protégé of Bernie Bierman, the great University of Minnesota football coach. Bierman was a proponent of power football. Coach Brockmeyer was a good student. His teams played power football!

Under normal circumstances Ashland and Wausau high schools would never compete in interscholastic athletic contests. The two cities were approximately 150 miles apart, and in that era, this was too far for teams to travel. Then fate intervened. During an informal get together at the annual Wisconsin High School Coaches Association meeting in Madison, Coach Brockmeyer happened to mention that he just got word that one of his football games was canceled due to the polio threat. Without missing a beat, Dad spoke up, "Why Brock, I have an opening. Come to Ashland and play us." As witnessed by the coaching group, details were quickly put in place for an Ashland–Wausau home and home series.

Dad had stretched the truth a bit as Ashland already had a game scheduled for the weekend of the proposed first game. With a call to Principal Mel Asher, the schedule was rearranged. The first Wausau game was set for the night of September 27, 1946 at Ashland, and the second at Wausau in 1949. The stage was set for one of the most memorable

Wisconsin high school football games of the twentieth century. Sixty years later football fans in northern Wisconsin still talk about the "Wausau game." Coach Brockmeyer had just another game. Dad had the challenge of his career!

What thoughts went through Dad's mind on the long trip back to Ashland? He had talked about playing Wausau for years and now he had not one, but two games scheduled. The first one in five weeks!

I don't know when Dad conceived the unique defense for the Wausau game. Was it on that long drive back to Ashland from the football clinic or had he developed the concepts earlier but never used them? I believe he formalized the defense on the trip home. If he had conceived the defense earlier, he surely would have used it against Superior Central and Ironwood who utilized a single wing formation similar to Wausau's offense.

Dad's Wausau defensive scheme was not evolutionary; it was revolutionary. His defense was totally different from the established defenses used against the single wing offense. The normal defenses were 6-2-2-1 or 7-2-2 alignments with the linemen charging straight ahead to penetrate the offensive line. This was mass against mass, power against power! The strongest team usually won.

Dad's concept used finesse and variation to confuse and befuddle the opponents, through various combinations of straight and slashing charges. Coach called it "shooting the gap," the forerunner to blitzing which is so popular today. This may very well have been the first formalization of the concept of blitzing. In the National Football League the concept of blitzing, called red dogging, named after Don "Red Dog" Ettinger of the New York Giants, didn't emerge as a defensive team concept until the 1950s.

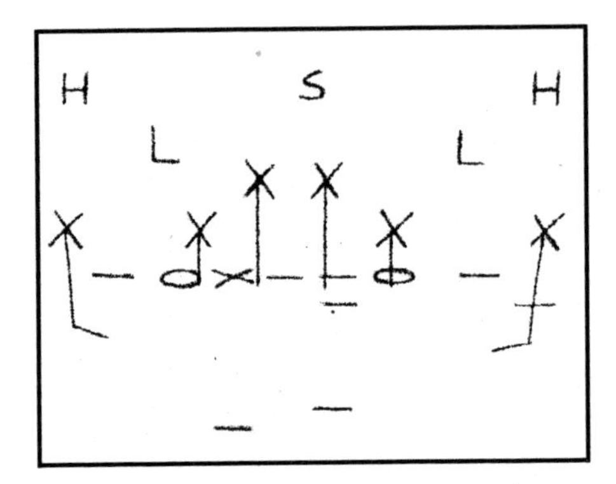

Diagram # 8 – Basic Alignment "Shooting the Gap" Defenses

Dad kept talking about immobilizing the Wausau linemen. I didn't understand what he meant by immobilizing. Was he going to embed their feet in concrete?

His defense included four basic plays from a 4-2-2-2-1 alignment. This alignment appeared as a four man line, which was unheard of in the 1940s. It really amounted to a six man line because, in all four plays, the four linemen and two inside linebackers crossed the line of scrimmage in varying charging patterns. This variation of charging was designed to confuse and immobilize the opponent.

Dad's game strategy was to make Wausau move the ball long distances. His offensive plan was conservative and relied on the "punting game to put Wausau deep into their territory." He believed the game would be low scoring. One or two touchdowns could win the game.

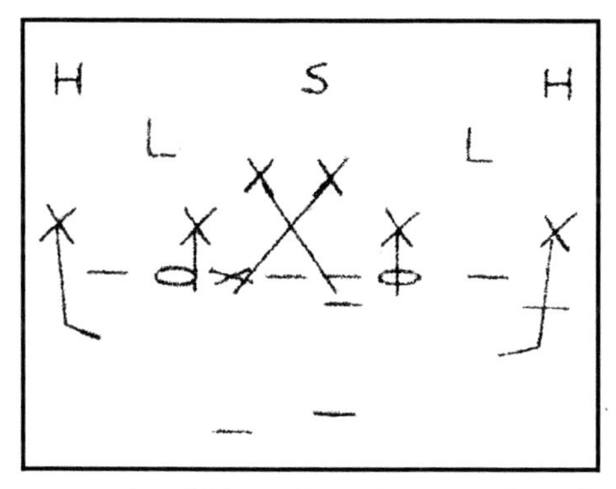

Diagram #9 – "Shooting the Gap" – Play #1
In Play #1 the inside linebackers crisscross

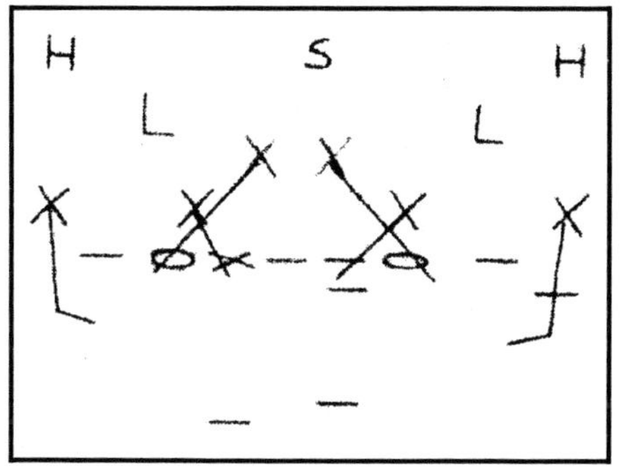

Diagram #10 – "Shooting the Gap" – Play #2
In Play #2 the inside linebackers flare out and tackles crash in.

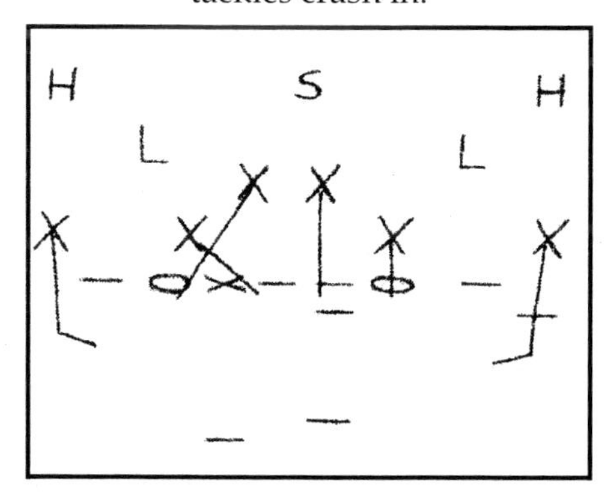

Diagram #11 – "Shooting the Gap" – Play #3
In Play #3 the right inside linebacker and tackle crisscross.

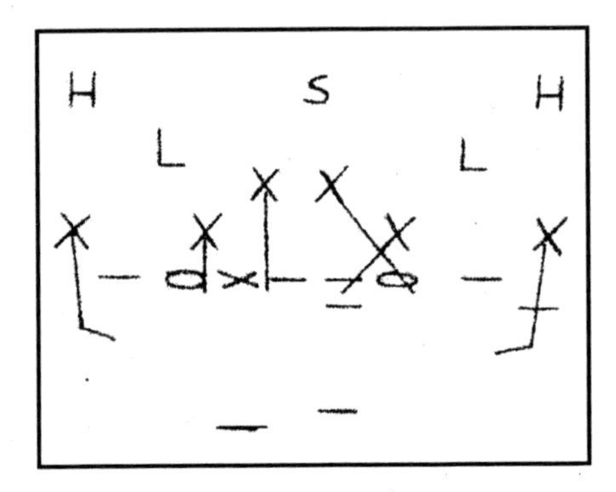

Diagram #12 -"Shooting the Gap" - Play #4
Play #4 is a mirror image of Play #3 with the left inside linebacker and tacklers crisscrossing.

I became enthused by his talk and concepts. It all looked good on paper with the "Xs" and "Os" and arrows going in every direction and the talk about finessing and immobilizing. I forgot about Wausau's size, depth, and talent. I forgot about the ten year record -- the sixty-nine games without a defeat.

Few others forgot and even fewer believed Ashland had any chance of winning. Ashland might put up a good game but, in the end, Wausau would win. I'm sure Dad had no illusions. Wausau was a formidable team, with great coaching and traditions, comparable to the Ironwood and Bessemer teams of the 1920s and 1930s.

The 1946 Wausau team was a typical Win Brockmeyer team: a team with large, well schooled linemen, and two outstanding backs, David Bleisee and Rollie Strahlow. These two backs in tandem were better than the usual backs on the Wausau teams. This hard hitting Wausau team was disciplined and fundamentally sound. In a word, they were an offensive and defensive powerhouse! We were the decided underdog. We were David against Goliath.

Being the underdog and being outclassed was not new to Coach. Coach had a special defense and a couple of surprise offensive plays. He had a veteran team, bigger and more talented than usual. The regulars could probably hold their own against the Wausau eleven. But Wausau had depth (second and third team players capable of playing), particularly in linemen, and Ashland didn't. We were in for a long struggle.

Coach altered his normal pre-season practice routine. Usually he devoted the majority of time to installing the offense. This year everything was geared to the new defense for the Wausau game, even though there were games with Hurley and Park Falls before Wausau came to town. He could afford this change in training procedure because he had a veteran team familiar with the offense. He did, however, install two new offensive plays to take advantage of David Bleisee's aggressive nature. His game plan relied on this new defense and a conservative offense with emphasis on the kicking (punting) game.

We won our first two games, beating Hurley 12 – 7 and Park Falls 6 – 0. We won, but we looked poor in both wins and we lost Ed Ziolkowski and Ken Tidstrom to injuries. This was a huge blow. Ziolkowski was an outstanding blocker and was the key left outside linebacker on our new defense. Wausau won their opening game with Marshfield, 20 – 0.

During the week prior to the game, Dad had last minute doubts about the new defense. After all, it had never been tried. He didn't use it against either Hurley or Park Falls. Years later he told me he didn't sleep that Wednesday night before the Wausau game, thinking about the defense - thinking maybe he should scrap it for a more conventional defense. But time was running out. It was too late for doubts.

Wausau would be here Friday night! There is an old saying, "Be careful what you wish for, you may get it." Since the Hurley days Dad had wanted a game with Wausau. Now he had it!

That September night was perfect for football. People came from all over northern Wisconsin and the Range to see Ashland take on the Wausau Lumberjacks. It was the largest crowd I had ever seen at an Ashland High School football game. There were as many people standing as were sitting in the stands. Some were even sitting atop the five foot chain link fence that enclosed the field.

We were already on the field doing pre-game warm-ups when the Wausau players appeared. From the darkened practice area, they entered the field running single file. Instead of assembling on their half of the field, they began running around the perimeter of the field, a player stopping at five yard increments. I started counting them 1 ... 2 ... 10 ... 25 ... 45 ... 60! They encircled the entire field and us. We were surrounded! Our team just stood around and gawked. We'd never seen a traveling squad of sixty players. No wonder they had arrived in a rented Greyhound bus. No little yellow school bus could hold them. Then, on signal, they broke ranks and reassembled on their half of the field in rows and columns. Supervised by numerous coaches, they conducted military style calisthenics. The bright lights glinted off their silver helmets like stars and I started thinking. "They're so many ... they're so big ... they're going to make us 'see stars'!" Then the Wausau squad divided into five teams and ran offensive plays to loud cadences. They looked like the New York Giants' football team. We looked like dwarfs. The only thing missing from this warm-up spectacular was the blare of trumpets. Wausau's pre-game warm-up performance was meant to intimidate us. It did! At least it intimidated me.

In my mind I knew that no one, on or off the field, could possibly believe that we had a chance of winning; no one except Dad. Even if Ed Ziolkowski and Ken Tidstrom could have played, I didn't think we could ever beat these giants. I was suited up, but I was just a freshman. I was glad I wouldn't be playing.

The game itself actually followed the script Coach had outlined. Wausau got the ball deep, moved it some, was stopped by Ashland's defense, or punted to Ashland. Ashland couldn't advance the ball, punted (sometimes quick kicked) the ball deep into Wausau territory, gaining yardage on most exchanges. This process repeated itself over and over. The defense did its job. The Wausau linemen were clearly confused. The smaller Ashland defenders frequently were in the Wausau backfield, disrupting the plays. The first quarter ended in a 0 to 0 tie.

The second quarter was a repeat of the first, except Wausau's fullback, Bliesee, scored on a thirty yard run up the middle. On this play every player, except Bliesee, was on the ground — a testament to the Wausau blocking prowess. It was as if a bomb had exploded leveling everyone on the field, except the ball carrier and the referees. Wausau clearly outplayed Ashland in the second quarter. Their size and depth began to control the game. At half time the teams left the field, with Wausau leading 7 to 0.

Coach was a very good half time coach. He usually made play and position adjustments, offered encouragement, attended to minor injuries and occasionally utilized Knute Rockne-type psychology. This half time was different. Wausau was using our locker room in Dodd Gym. Exhausted, we were sitting or lying on the floor in the main hall of the

Latimar Building, our makeshift locker room. It was quiet. The team was tired. We were just waiting for Coach. Finally he entered the hallway. He started yelling at the team and, in particular, at Charlie Yderstad. Charlie had played outstandingly. I was shocked. I'd never seen Coach act like this. He always seemed to be in control. I was embarrassed. The team had played a tremendous game against a larger opponent. They had executed his game plan perfectly. What had gotten into him?

Then he left the makeshift locker room. The players were furious. Years later, I asked Dad about that half time. He said that it was a psychological ploy to get them mad at him and to have that anger transfer against the opposing team.

We trudged out for the second half, behind 7 to 0. If we hadn't scored in the first half, when we were fresh, I didn't know how we could score in the second half. Wausau's power was taking its toll. They were slowly wearing us down.

In the third quarter Coach continued to play the first of two new offensive plays designed specifically for Wausau. The first play was a fake draw to the tailback and a pitchout to the fullback going to our strong side and away from their weak side linebacker David Bliesee. Bliesee was not only big and strong, he was very aggressive. Coach had designed this play to encourage him to chase our fullback who was running around the strong side away from Bliesee. Because of this play, Bliesee wasn't seeing much defensive action, so, by the third quarter, he took the bait and started chasing the play, thus taking himself out of position. Late in the third quarter, with the ball on Wausau's twenty-six yard line, Coach signaled for the second play.

The second play started exactly like the first play. Bob

Howard faked a hand-off to tailback Fred Tidstrom, faked a pitch out to the fullback, stepped back and threw a pass to Tidstrom who had run into the zone covered by Bliesee. But David Bliesee wasn't there. He was chasing the fake pitch out. Fred Tidstrom caught the pass, and all alone, ran unobstructed for a touchdown. Marvin Hunt kicked the extra point and the third quarter ended in a 7 to 7 tie. Incredibly Coach had done it again! All night long his defense baffled the Wausau linemen and now his two new offensive plays finessed their great linebacker.

But there was a whole quarter to go. Could the tired Ashland team hold on? We had few substitutes; Wausau, sixty strong, rotated many of their players. Our same exhausted eleven players had to finish the game while Wausau's players got some rest. Their depth of material was a big advantage. Would it tell in the fourth quarter?

The fourth quarter was a repeat of the first quarter. Ball possession seesawed back and forth. Twice Ashland stopped Wausau inside Ashland's five yard line.

Toward the end of the game, Ashland kicked the football deep into Wausau's territory. Wausau only advanced the ball to their twenty-six yard line. With a tied score, just one minute to play, and fourth down, Wausau was forced to punt. Charlie Yderstad blocked Rollie Strehlow's punt. Dave Suminski picked up the ball and ran twenty yards for a touchdown. Ashland's missed extra point was anticlimactic. Ashland led 13 to 7, with just seconds left to play!

On the first play after the ensuing kickoff, Wausau attempted a pass. Bobby Howard intercepted it. The game ended with the ball, and the game, in Ashland's hands. This weary band of Ashland players had pulled off the biggest upset in Wisconsin High School football history. The *Wausau*

Daily Record-Herald said:

> Roy E. Melvin, a former Wausau high school athlete, is the coach of the Oredockers, a team that cut a winning skein no other high school team in these United States had paralleled or equaled, according to stories which have been printed in newspapers within the last year.

The game was an even match. The difference was a blocked punt. The statistics favored Wausau, but statistics don't win games.

STATISTICS	WAUSAU	ASHLAND
First downs	12	6
Rushing yards	208 yds	7 yds
Passes attempted	6	10
Passes completed	0	7
Passing yards	0 yds	77 yds
Total yards	208 yds	84 yds
Punts	2	6
Punting yards	55 yds	270 yds
Punting average	27.5 yds	45 yds
Fumbles	4`	1
Fumbles recovered	2	3
Penalty yards	5 yds	5 yds

Note the differences in punting yardage:
Ashland gained 215 yards on punting, approximately three times their total running and passing yardage

The game was played as Coach envisioned. Wausau's offense was stymied by Ashland's defense and good kicking game. The Ashland team played the game of their lives. Jim Goeltz writing in the *Ashland Daily Press* said:

> Personally, the 13-7 whipping Ashland gave Wausau, was the sweetest game I've ever seen on a high school gridiron. Almost everything the 'Dockers tried clicked. The line charged brilliantly. The backfield although without Ed Ziolkowski was in perfect coordination and timing, and the way that Ashland line charged the Lumberjacks front wall, you'd think that the locals had the edge in beef instead of Wausau. Wausau, you know, had about a 30 pound edge in the line and a 20 pound edge in the backfield.

I wouldn't say Ashland gave Wausau a whipping, but we did snap Wausau's ten year winning streak.

The 1946 Ashland "Giant killers"

This Ashland team played a fantastic game. Without

Coach's defensive scheme I doubt if Ashland would have prevailed. To the Wausau team and coaches the defense was confusing and complex, just what Coach had intended. To the individual Ashland player, however, it was pure simplicity. In the four defensive plays utilized, each player had a single assignment and every player was active on every play. There was nothing complex about that. The totality of these simple individual assignments created the complexity. The Wizard of the North Woods had worked his magic!

THREE YEARS LATER THREE HEAD COACHES INTENSELY SCRUTINIZED Ashland's 1949 season opener against Park Falls. Two were on the field: Coach with his Oredockers and Park Falls' John MacDonald with his Cardinals. One was in the stands, Coach Win Brockmeyer of the Wausau Lumberjacks. It was our year to "pay the piper" with a return game on Wausau's turf. Coach Brockmeyer and his entire coaching staff were in Park Falls to scout this game. This could be taken as quite a compliment to Coach Melvin and his little band of players. Although Wausau's coaching staff saw us play a sloppy game and come out on the short end of a 7 – 6 game, they weren't taking Ashland High School for granted this time.

We weren't taking Wausau lightly either! Wausau hadn't lost a game since its 1946 loss to Ashland. They were now approaching one hundred wins marred only by that one loss to us. In one week we would be traveling to Wausau for the much talked about rematch. Both teams were fundamentally sound but neither equaled the 1946 squads. Ashland had a small veteran squad, lacking size and depth. Wausau had their usual size and depth.

Coach had another surprise in store for Wausau. His defensive formation looked like a standard 7-2-2 defense but it really was a 9-2 defense because two linebackers were assigned to eliminate the Wausau blockers and the two defensive backs were left to make the tackles. This was a totally different defensive approach from the 1946 game. This was power against power and we got "our power" by having nine players on or near the line of scrimmage. Offensively, Coach would use his modified T-formation offense without the reverse quarterback. We would use the single wing plays exclusively, so we could pass from the tailback position. As in the 1946 game, punting would again be an important aspect of our game plan.

This was the first overnight trip for a football game in the history of Ashland High School. We left Ashland early on Friday morning and, after a four and a half hour bus trip, checked into the Wausau Hotel. After an early dinner we were off to Wausau High School.

Pre-game locker room procedures were quite normal. Pre-game warm-up on the field was far from normal. When we entered the stadium we were greeted by 5,000 to 6,000 rabid Wausau fans. The boos and noise were deafening. Revenge was in the air! I wasn't intimidated, nor were any of my teammates, but we knew we were in for a tough game. This game was played on Wausau's turf and to Wausau's tune. The stronger team would win.

The first quarter was played to a scoreless tie and the tone of the game was fairly well set. Early in the game it was apparent that we couldn't establish a running game. Passing and punting would have to carry our offense. Wausau had a reputation as a powerful offensive team, but their defense was just as strong. They simply came at you both offensively and defensively. It was obvious that their game plan was to wear us down. They had the size and depth to do it, and were highly successful at it, as their record proved. So why change?

Early in the second quarter we exploited Wausau's susceptibility to deception plays and scored a touchdown on a delayed pass play. We led at half-time 6 to 0. On the downside, Wausau was winning the battle of attrition. Their strategy of changing their entire line at every change of ball possession was taking its toll. Since we had few adequate substitutes our original eleven played most of the first half. The game was beginning to be a battle of time. Could we hold out for another twenty-four minutes?

Coach made no adjustments at half time nor did he have any psychological ploys. I think he knew we were giving all we had. We were! We seldom got an open shot at the ball carriers. We couldn't get clean tackles. We were making tackles over downed Wausau blockers or Ashland linebackers. Frustration was high!

The third quarter was scoreless. The game of attrition and time continued. We had two regulars out with injuries and a couple of others banged up. Larry Hinds, our center, was "out on his feet" but there was no one to replace him. You simply couldn't put fourteen and fifteen year olds against these larger, experienced Wausau linemen. Our subs were inexperienced and not familiar with all the offensive plays.

By the fourth quarter Wausau was gaining control of the game. Each time they had possession they penetrated deeper into our territory. Could we hold out for another twelve minutes? With approximately eight minutes remaining, we gained possession of the ball on our ten yard line and on the first play fumbled the ball. Wausau recovered! Whether we fumbled because of our tiredness or Wausau's aggressive play doesn't matter. Wausau scored in the next series of plays. They attempted the extra point by running and we were able to stop them. The score was 6 to 6 with a little over six minutes remaining. On the ensuing kick off we returned the ball to about our thirty yard line.

Coach always left the play calling to the players and in this case I was responsible for offensive plays. I figured we had to take as much time off the clock as we could so I planned to call two running plays followed by the pass play that had given us a touchdown earlier in the game. If the pass play was successful we would continue the time consuming strategy. If it wasn't we would punt the ball deep into Wausau's territory and hope to hold on to preserve a 6 to 6 tie.

We ran two plays to the right. On the third down I called the pass play. This play required a fake to the right with a back delaying one count and slipping though the line into the short side flats. Because of the time required to execute the play the outside right guard was to pull out and block on the left side. Unfortunately, the outside guard was a substitute player and didn't know he was to pull out. When I turned to the short side to throw the pass the receiver was wide open with nobody near him or between him and the goal line. However, the big right defensive end was bearing down on me. I threw the pass. It was tipped into the air. The end knocked me down and the defensive tackle on that side caught the deflected pass and ran for a touchdown. What emotional gas we had left was just drained out. We had nothing left. Wausau scored the extra point and led 13 to 6. The game was over but time remained. Anticlimactically, Wausau scored again, winning 20 – 6.

Up until the tipped pass I thought we had a chance to win or at least tie the game. Superior size and depth finally prevailed. If the game had been sixty minutes, the score may very well have been 66 — 6. The "Wizard of the North Woods" didn't have enough tricks this time. We had done everything he had asked! We had played hard, clean football. We could hold our heads high. Wausau would go on winning and the Wizard and his little band of players retreated to the North Woods to regroup.

I don't remember much about the time after the game. I was too tired to be disappointed. I do remember returning to the Wausau Hotel and soaking in a hot bath for about an hour. Maybe my tired feelings had something to do with the Wausau newspaper's report that "Brockmeyer is particularly concerned about the passing attack led by Stu Melvin," and his prediction that "I would be a marked man." I just knew that the next day was a long trip back to Ashland.

In retrospect, it was a valiant game. But for an inexperienced young lineman not knowing his assignment, we would have tied or won the game. On the other hand, it was just a game and we did our best, which was all Coach ever asked. Even the Wausau press acknowledged:

> To Ashland's credit, it must be said that it was as game a team as will be seen here this year. But when you scan the injury list of one broken nose, one shoulder separation, a pulled leg muscle and several boys with the wind knocked out of their sails, it's easy to see why the Oredockers were a beaten team in the final minutes of the game.

Roy Melvin, head Coach of the 1948
North All-Star Football Team with his
assistants, Whitey Ketelaar (left)
and Tony Ellis (right)

CHAPTER 10

THE ALL-STAR FOOTBALL GAME
1948

FOR COACH, THE FOOTBALL YEAR STARTED before the season began! His realm shifted from the small towns of northern Wisconsin to a statewide arena. For me, I morphed from the coach's son to "shadow coach."

In 1946 the Wisconsin High School Coaches Association, as part of their efforts to develop a wider interest in high school sports, started sponsorship of an annual high school all-star football game. They divided the state into North and South squads selected from the previous spring's high school graduates. This North-South All-Star Game was popular with the coaches, players and fans, but was opposed by the Wisconsin Interscholastic Athletic Association (WIAA) and later by the Big Ten Board of Control. The game was ultimately discontinued and reinstated in 1977 as the Shrine All-Star Game.

The South won the first two games played at the University of Wisconsin's Camp Randall Stadium. In the first match-up Coach Lisle Blackbourn from Milwaukee's Washington High led the South All-Stars to a 20 – 6 victory over the North All-Stars coached by Wausau's Win Brockmeyer. The next year the South All-Stars coached by Walter "Wadz" Martens from Darlington came away with another easy 31 – 6 victory over the North All-Stars, coached by Superior Central's Harry Conley.

During the August 1947 Wisconsin High School Coaches Association meeting there was little opposition in deciding to move the future games from Camp Randall to Beese Stevens Field in Madison. There was a lot of discussion, however, about the South's perceived dominance. Talk of moving the North-South dividing line further south surfaced. In order to achieve a fifty percent population split, the original line was already very close to the Illinois border. It started in Prairie du Chien, Wisconsin on the Mississippi River, ran east along U.S. Highway 18 to Madison, north around Lake Mendota to U.S. Highway 151, northeast to Beaver Dam and then east to Lake Michigan, actually splitting metropolitan Milwaukee. (See map on page 13) Talk about shifting boundaries ended when someone suggested, "Let Mel coach the North squad. If he can't win, then maybe the line should be adjusted."

Five hundred plus coaches chose Dad as the 1948 head coach of the North All-Stars and Ken Kitelinger from Janesville as coach of the South All-Stars. Dad's two assistants, selected by the coaches, were Tony Ellis and Whitey Ketelaar, both highly successful football coaches.

By their nature, all-star games are difficult for both the players and the coaches. The players don't know one another, the coaches or the coach's system. The coaches don't know one another nor do they know the players. The assistants don't know the head coach's system, its nomenclatures or idiosyncrasies. No one knows the opponents. To further complicate the situation, there is limited time to prepare. The only good thing is that both squads have the same problems.

Despite these difficulties, Dad had one advantage that Coach Kitelinger didn't. He had a third coach, a "shadow coach"- me! Dad invited me to attend the training camp and it became my first and only "coaching experience." I was thrilled! For the first time I would be privy to the total picture from start to finish: his concepts, thoughts and strategies. I would get a complete insight into his thinking and his approach to this rather unique coaching experience.

Dad had only five weeks to prepare for the first Wausau battle; now he had almost a year to prepare for Ken Kitelinger's South team. But first there was the 1947-1948 football, basketball, track, and tennis seasons. The All-Star game went on the back burner until June.

When June finally arrived, the game was uppermost in Dad's mind. South's Coach Kenny Kitelinger was expected to play a standard T-formation. Dad planned to install his modified T-formation. The newspapers started talking about Roy Melvin's "cockeyed T-formation."

Dad wasn't thinking about the "T" or offense. Defense was on his mind! On the long two hundred mile drive to the Stevens Point training camp, he discussed with me his game strategy and his defensive concepts. He didn't know much about his thirty all-stars except for the reputations of Pat O'Donahue and Gene Felker, whose talent he planned to use with his defensive scheme and Rollie Strehlow from Wausau, his main offensive threat.

Upon arriving in Stevens Point that weekend Dad checked out the facility and the housekeeping arrangements. Nothing was said about the shadows coach's role.

All his talk was defense. His defense was designed to smother a standard T-formation. How do you smother a formation? He outlined his concept to me. He would use his five interior defensive linemen to "pinch in" the South's five interior offensive linemen. This would place ten large bodies in the space originally occupied by the five interior offensive linemen, effectively sealing any holes at the line of scrimmage. In other words, jamming the middle and forcing all runners to the outside.

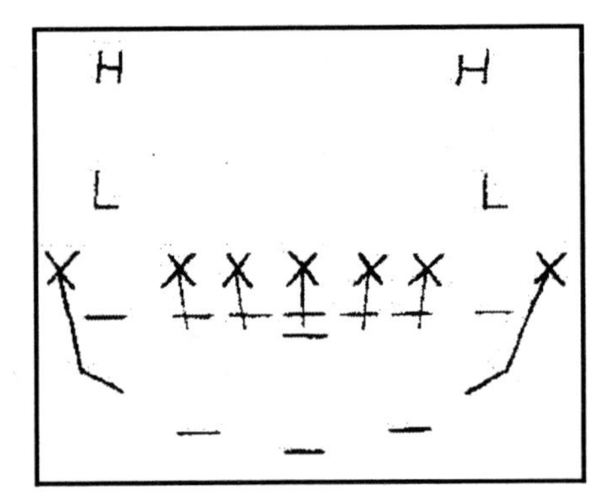

Diagram #13 – North's Defensive Alignment

As with the Wausau defense of two years ago, Dad's defensive concept was revolutionary, consisting of four plays from the basic defensive alignment.

In all four defensive plays (Diagrams 14-17) the defensive linemen created a "log jam" of players, by playing on the outside shoulder of the offensive linemen and charging inward on a slant. If the North linemen broke through they made a tackle or sacked the passers; if they didn't, all holes were sealed off. The interior linemen would pinch in, and the ends and linebackers would blitz to create a nine man line. The opponents would be smothered. Coach promised, "We'll be in their backfield all night."

But what about stopping the pass? To Coach it was simple. "We'll be all over the passer before he can throw." The defensive halfback (H) on each side would cover the ends, and the outside blitzers would pick up any backs trying to get into the flats for a pass reception.

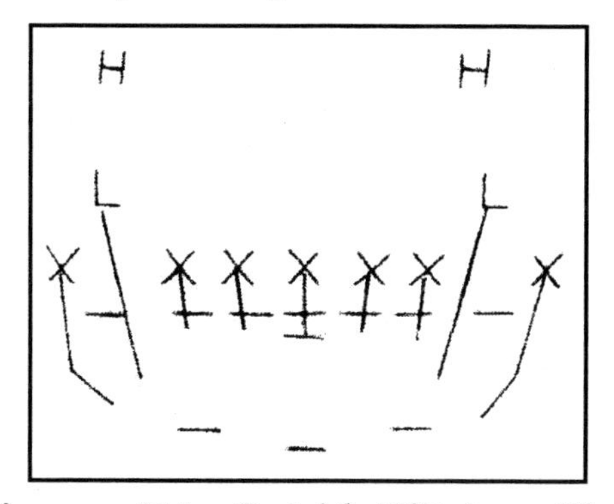

Diagram #14 – Outside Blitzing – Play #1

Play #1 is a double outside blitz from both sides with the defensive ends responsible for any backs coming out of the backfield.

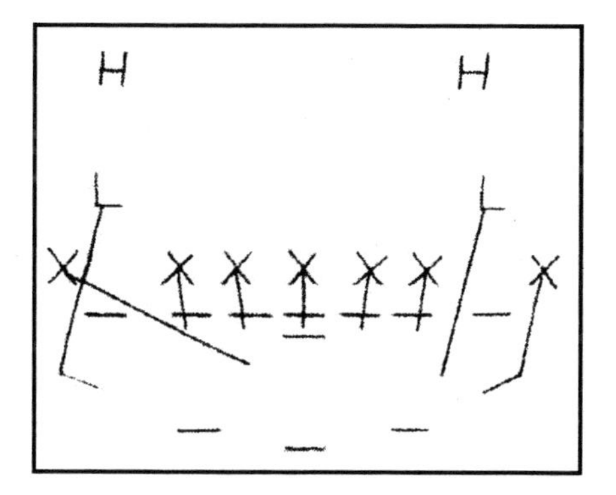

Diagram #15 – Outside Blitzing – Play #2

Play #2 is a double outside blitz from both sides with the right end crashing in on the quarterback.

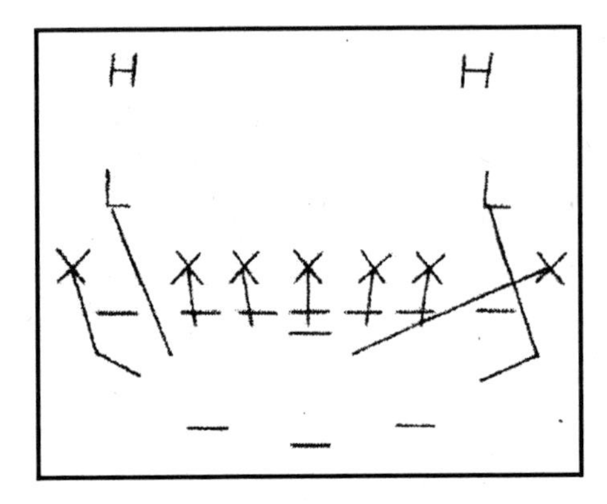

Diagram #16 – Outside Blitzing – Play #3
Play #3 is a mirror image of Play #2 with the left defensive end crashing in on the quarterback.

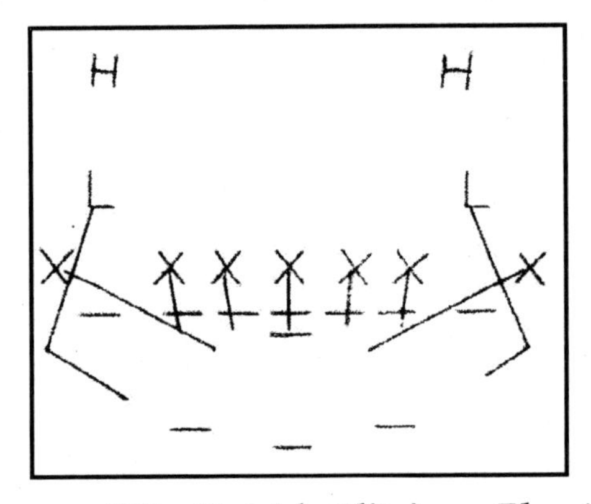

Diagram #17 – Outside Blitzing – Play #4
Play #4 is a double outside blitz from both sides with both defensive ends crashing in on the quarterback.

To successfully execute these four defensive plays, the five interior defensive linemen were key. For the first and only time in his coaching career Dad had a whole parcel of 190-210 pound linemen. In training camp he'd pick out his best five. Dad told me, "They will be the unsung heroes of North's game." Every defensive player would be active on every play. Simplicity and engagement were the cornerstones of his game strategy.

On Monday morning the squad got their equipment and started to get to know each other. While these activities were going on, he had a long private meeting with his two assistant coaches, Ellis and Ketelaar. Towards the end of Monday morning Coach called the team together, introduced his two assistants and addressed the squad.

Coach was at his best when he stood in front of players and faced a challenge. Although he didn't subscribe to the philosophy, "that winning was everything," he always believed that his team could win. At no time was his confidence to play a bigger role than in this game. I sensed that his talk of "being in the South's backfield all night" won the team's heart.

The 1948 North All-Star team

Could he convince them that his concepts and strategy would work? After all, most of these players had never seen Coach. Of the thirty players on this squad, only Harry Josewicz had played for him; only Joe Dida from Superior East, Joe Morgan from Park Falls and Rollie Strehlow from Wausau had ever played against one of his teams. Josewicz was popular with the guys and I'm sure he helped the other players believe in Dad. Strehlow probably helped too, as he had been on the receiving end of Coach's defensive wizardry in the 1946 Ashland-Wausau game. Time was short. Dad would need all his persuasive powers.

Monday night he broached the subject of my helping with the offense, as he had to concentrate on the defense. Clearly he had talked to the assistant coaches prior to asking me, and, because I knew the offense better than anyone but Dad, the assistant coaches agreed. The next day Dad and Tony Ellis took the defense. Whitey Ketelaar took the offense, with me explaining the nomenclature and demonstrating the plays.

Coach Ketelaar and I set to work on the ball exchange from center to quarterback. The reverse quarterback was foreign to both the center and quarterback. We practiced the ball exchange until both center and quarterback were confident that they could consistently make the exchange. We NEVER installed the plays requiring the center to snap the ball through the quarterback's legs to the tailback or plays that set the quarterback in motion and required the center to snap the ball to a spinning fullback. We kept it simple, eliminating difficult center snaps and complex backfield movements and footwork. We only practiced a handful of "T" plays.

Blocking assignments for the linemen were our second offensive priority. By 1948 most high school coaches had installed the T-formation so many linemen were not familiar with single wing blocking techniques. Coach's modified T-formation utilized an unbalanced line and retained many of the blocking techniques of the single wing. We made our blocking job easier by eliminating all single wing plays. We concentrated on double team post blocks and Coach's concept of having the backs run directly at the offensive linemen and then cut into the hole that developed, rather than running into the gap (hole) between linemen. We installed only a few basic pass plays. We kept everything simple. Then Rollie Strehlow got injured in practice and couldn't play. He was our punting and passing threat. Yes, passing! Strehlow was a terrific passer even though under Coach Brockmeyer's system he didn't pass very often. I just hoped that we wouldn't have any offensive disasters during the game.

Coach paid scant attention to the offense and the punting game. He handled the defense and all the other things to prepare the squad for the game. For Coach the game was defense, defense, and more defense. He was going to win this game on defense alone. One touchdown would be enough. I believed him, but I wondered if anyone else did? I wasn't sure we could smother the South in their backfield, or that we could stop the pass every time, but I knew we were going to win or lose with the defense.

It was on to Madison and the game! Coach's winning confidence had imbued that entire squad. But would the team believe in the game strategy? Wednesday night at Beese Steven Field we would find out!

The newspaper accounts of the actual game painted a picture of a poor offensive showing, producing a slow and even boring game. One paper, noting that there probably wasn't sufficient time to develop the offense, did acknowledge: "the North's defense totally dominated the game." Of course, the newspaper reporters didn't know about Coach's defensive concept. Nor could they appreciate it because they hadn't seen "blitzing" before this game. It hadn't even been named.

In the hundreds of football games that I have seen in the last sixty years, I've never seen a defense so completely control the line of scrimmage. During the game I sometimes felt sorry for the South's backs. They never had a chance to see the daylight. We were in their backfield all night. We smothered them. It was no surprise to me that a defensive play by North's Gene Felker scored the game's only touchdown. On the second play of the game, Felker blitzed, intercepted a lateral and ran nineteen yards for the winning score. I knew then that the game was over! The outcome was never in doubt. The game was played almost exclusively in South's territory. North won the statistical battle and the game, 7 – 0. This was the first time the entire state had seen the Wizard of the North Woods in action.

Ashland's Harry Josewicz stops Ironwood; the Oredockers break Ironwood's 25 year winning streak over them, 1946

Hurley Midgets showing their hoop highs during the 1949 state championship game

CHAPTER 11

PIGSKIN POWER AND HOOP HIGHS
1946 to 1949

COACH'S IMAGINATIVE AND INNOVATIVE FOOTBALL STYLE made him known and respected among the coaches; his modified "T" football formation caught the attention of the sports writers throughout the state. It was his 1946 Wausau win and 1948 North-South All-Star win that elevated his reputation as a football coach to sports writers and fans throughout the state. It also propelled the careers of football players like Charlie Yderstad and Dave Suminski.

On the Range, Hurley's 1941 football win over Ironwood and Ashland's 1942 football win over Bessemer broke Michigan's football dominance in the Michigan-Wisconsin conference. In 1946 Coach's Ashland football team defeated Ironwood 15 - 6, breaking Ironwood's twenty-six-year winning streak against Ashland. That 1946 Ashland football team finished with a 6 – 1 record. Only the controversial 7 -- 6 loss to Superior Central stopped this great team from having an undefeated season. In this game Ashland had five, yes, five touchdowns called back. Ashland was robbed! I think the only mistake Dad made that football season was having two referees from Superior officiate the game. Needless to say they never officiated another Ashland game while Dad was at Ashland High School. The 1946 football season ended with Ashland winning the Michigan-Wisconsin Football Conference title for the first time. After years of Michigan dominance, finally Hurley and Ashland were winning football conference championships. This trend continued until the league was disbanded.

THE SPORTS' PROWESS OF THE HURLEY – ASHLAND DUO wasn't limited to pigskin power. Three appearances of North Wood's teams in the eight team state basketball finals, Hurley in 1943 and Ashland in 1945 and 1946, established high hoop expectations. Not a bad record, considering more than three hundred high schools of all sizes participated in these annual sudden death tournaments.

Big time basketball ushered in the second half of the '40s in the North Woods. The defending NBA Champion Minneapolis Lakers came to Dodd Gym to play an exhibition game against the Harlem Globetrotters. Fans packed Dodd Gym. Dad told me not to miss the half time show as one of the legends of the Globetrotters, Abe Gibson, would put on a shooting demonstration. When the teams retired for the half, none of the fans got out of their seats. The crowd waited. Nothing happened. Finally someone pushed a three and a half foot high and five foot diameter wire basket filled with basketballs onto the court. The fans waited. No one appeared.

At last a white-haired black man in the Globetrotter uniform shuffled onto the court and wandered the length of the gym aimlessly looking up at the girders. I was baffled. Dad had said that Abe Gibson was one of the great set shots of all time and that I should observe his shooting techniques. He looked so old and frail. I wondered if he could even shoot from the center line. Why did he keep walking and staring at the girders?

Finally he pushed the basket of balls to the top of the free throw circle, took a ball, bounced it a few times, and then turned his back to the basket and, with a flick of his wrist, shot the ball through two girders into the opposite basket some seventy feet away. The ball never touched the back board or the rim. He repeated this performance a number of times, bowed to the fans and shuffled off the floor. I don't remember the game, but I'll never forget his two-handed set shots.

The Laker-Globetrotter game gave the fans a one-time thrill. The strong competition among the northern basketball teams, led by the Hurley Midgets and the Ashland Oredockers, two programs indelibly shaped by one coach, gave fans game after game thrills.

DAD BELIEVED THAT TEAMS GOT BETTER the stronger the competition. The competitive nature of conference play was good for a team's development. Dad also liked to schedule non-conference games against good teams. In the pre-World War II era of tight money, long distance travel wasn't possible, so non-conference games were usually with "weak sisters" (smaller, nearby schools). After the war, Dad sought out the big schools within a 150 mile range. He had no trouble; he had wide connections with the state coaches through his long time involvement on the state rules committee and his active participation in the Wisconsin High School Coaches Association.

Dad especially liked to get games with teams from the strong Wisconsin Valley Conference. The Christmas holiday four game basketball round robin between the Hurley and Ashland teams and Merrill and Antigo of the Wisconsin Valley Conference became a post war tradition and a team favorite. Hurley and Ashland never lost. Some years Dad was successful in scheduling match-ups with other tough Wisconsin Valley teams. In all the 1940s basketball match-ups with Wisconsin Valley teams, Hurley and Ashland held a 14 - 0 record.

Christmas vacations provided Dad the opportunity to scrimmage his current team against players from previous teams. These scrimmages provided great competition and interesting results. One Christmas we scrimmaged a strong Northland College team. In this case, we gave them a drubbing. Another year we played against a group from the great 1944-45 team and they gave us a real lesson in basketball. They showed us how basketball should be played. Their passing and rebound were awesome and their defensive play shut down our scoring machine.

IN 1946-47 HURLEY FINISHED the regular season with a 16–1 record, defeating a powerful Bessemer team twice to win the Michigan-Wisconsin conference championship. In the regional tournament held at Superior Central, Hurley stalled the last two and a half minutes to barely beat a so-so Ashland team for the championship. There was no shot clock in those days. In the first game of the state finals the Midgets beat number one ranked Stevens Point 51–30. Hurley eventually placed second in the state, losing the championship game to a strong Beloit team. Hurley finished the season with a 22–2 record.

THE 1947-48 BASKETBALL SEASON featured a strong competitive field. Bessemer and Hurley had good squads; Superior Central, Superior East and Ashland weren't too bad. In regional tournament play Hurley and Ashland battled in Dodd Gym for the regional title game. Hurley was the favorite. The game was sold out and approximately half the fans were from Hurley.

With a minute or two remaining, Ashland led this hard fought game by five points. Then the game turned into a melee. The official froze and lost control of the game. At one point all ten players were on the floor after a loose ball and no whistle was blown. The most egregious officiating occurred when Hurley's Carl Hermanson received a mid-court inbound pass over his shoulder and ran the remaining distance without dribbling. He literally ran with the ball for about forty-five feet before he made a lay up shot. The whistle didn't blow! The officials didn't call traveling! We lost the game 30 – 29!

Hurley went on to the state tournament. They didn't win. Wauwatosa, with an undefeated record and with four of their five starters slated to return next year, won the state championship. Hurley went on to finish third in the Wisconsin state basketball finals. What a banner year for North Woods basketball: Bessemer placed second in the Michigan State Basketball Class B Tournament and Hurley placed third in the Wisconsin State Basketball Tournament.

IN 1948-1949 there were probably more good basketball

teams in northern Wisconsin than during any other season of the 1940s. Superior Central was one of the best in the state. Hurley had a veteran team, headed by Carl Hermanson and Len Bartolutti and a good supporting cast. Superior East's veteran crew boasted outstanding rebounding and defense. Early in the season Ashland, the least experienced team, lost its most experienced player, Dick "Mouse" Miller because of the age eligibility rule. It's hard to determine the impact of his loss, but his unique driving ability and shooting skills added a great dimension to Coach's team. He was missed!

The regional tournament again showcased this aggregate strength. Central and Hurley had the strongest records. Central was favored, but Hurley had home court advantage. Interest in this tournament was intense. The doors closed a good hour before the start of the first game. Fans packed the gym, some literally sitting on the rafters.

In the opening round, Superior Central and Ashland seesawed right up to the end, with Central finally winning 36 – 34. With seconds remaining in the Hurley – Superior East game, Peter Savant's impossible shot from behind the blackboard gave Hurley a 38 – 36 victory. Only Savant could make that shot. His basketball set shot looked like a shot-put, with the ball starting out from the top of his shoulder, going almost straight up in a high arc, and descending to the basket. He was amazingly accurate with this shot.

The fans got their money's worth with these two games and came back Friday night for two more terrific games. In the Ashland - East contest John McDermott's last second shot sealed a 31 – 29 Ashland victory. Hurley played Central in the second game with the winner practically assured a subsequent berth in the state tournament in Madison. Going into the fourth quarter Central had a significant lead.

Superior's Don Polgase was devastating the Hurley defense. Hurley finally shifted Len Bartolutti to guard Polglase. Bartolutti held Polglase scoreless in the fourth quarter and the Midgets squeezed out a 38 – 37 victory. Hurley was going on to the sectional; we were going home! But what a regional tournament it had been! As in 1946, four games were decided by a total of seven points.

Hurley easily won the sectional tournament. For the third straight year they were on their way to Madison—on their way as definite underdogs. Wauwatosa, undefeated and the defending state champion, had a two year winning record of 38 -- 0.

In the first round Wauwatosa played the highly regarded and unbeaten Wisconsin Rapid's team in a game that many felt would decide the state championship. Wauwatosa won 55 – 49. In that same round Hurley, using only five players, beat Reedsburg 48 – 44 to advance to the semi-finals against 'Tosa. Wauwatosa, now at 39 -- 0, was the odds-on favorite to win the title for a second year. Hurley was given no chance to win. The headlines the next day shouted, **HURLEY HALTS 'TOSA WIN STREAK AT 39.** Improbable as it seems, the game was a no contest. Hurley won 62 – 50! They played their entire traveling squad.

Saturday night's state championship game pitted Hurley against LaCrosse Logan. Could Hurley repeat Reedsville's miracle of a few years ago? The Hurley Midgets, with only three players barely 6′ and two others around 5′8″or 5′9″, faced a much larger team lead by 6′7″ Jim Thomas. Last year Hurley had beaten Logan 48 – 30 to take third place in the state tournatment. Could they do it again? This was another year. This was for all the marbles.

The game was anything but anticlimactic. Hurley won a hard fought game 37 – 36. The Hurley Midgets were the number one basketball team in the state.

Dad was as happy as any Hurley fan. Finally, after six trips to the state tournament, the "North Woods' Duo" had their first state basketball title!

The 1949 Hurley Midget state basketball champion team
"The Team That Did!"
Top Row: Anonich, Tocci, Rainaldo, Martino , Coack Vergamini
Bottom Row: Matta, Hermanson, Savant, Barren, Bartolutti

To the undiscerning fan, the Hurley Midgets were an unlikely team to be state champions. Hurley didn't have a dominant player like Dick Axness, Bud Grant or Bones Hulmer. Nor did they have a great all-round player like Don Dick or Bruce Fossum. They did have tough competition. Many felt they were fortunate to survive that year's regional tournament. I have long thought the 1949 regional tournament had the best overall teams ever to have played in this northern regional tournament. The state tournament teams were outstanding. Both Wauwatosa and Wisconsin Rapids entered the tournament undefeated. LaCrosse Logan and Reedsburg had strong squads.

If they had tough competition and no great players, what did they have? The Midgets were a team in the finest sense of the word. As a team they were better than the sum of their individual players. To win an eight game sudden-death tournament with over three hundred competitors takes a team.

THE 1949-1950 basketball season started out on an optimistic note. Ashland had three returning starters and eight out of ten players from last year's squad. Five seniors were slated for the starting five.

The competition was much weaker than last year. Only Superior Central and Ashland had strong returning groups of players. Hurley and Superior East had lost their starting fives. Bones Hulmer, probably the best player in the state, was back for his senior year at DePadua where he, unfortunately, lacked a supporting cast.

Our preseason practice was chaotic. This was supposed to be a great basketball year. Instead Coach had a team that was disorganized and demoralized. All of the starting five had been on the football team. We were beat up physically and psychologically from the football season.

During the week of our first game, practices reached a crisis. On Tuesday, Coach called a halt, assembled the team, and told us to take a shower and go home. Tomorrow we were to either turn in our uniforms or show up for practice prepared to play his way.

I had no idea if anyone would show up for Wednesday's practice. I didn't even know if I would. There was practically no talk in the showers. Wednesday after school I headed to the gym. To my surprise everyone else did too.

Coach told us that there was no starting five. Every starting position was open to be won. He divided the squad into two roughly equal groups for very long scrimmages on Wednesday and Thursday. We still didn't know who would be starting.

The situation was contrary to Coach's normal procedures. He liked to have his starting five set and playing together at least two weeks before the first game. Friday's opening game was at home. Coach announced his starting five in the locker room just before the start of the game. They were the same as the first two weeks of practice. Coach gave no instructions for the game.

His psychology worked and we easily won our first four games. These first games established us as a high scoring team. Our fifth game was at Superior Central and we would find out how good we were. We weren't as good as we looked. Central won the high scoring game by the margin of home court advantage.

In our first game of the season with DePadua, our cross-town rival, Coach put in a defense to stop Bones Hulmer. He reasoned correctly that if Bones got the ball we couldn't stop him. So, for the first and only time, Coach instituted a pressing defense. We pressed the DePadua guards, kept the ball out of Bones' hands and won easily, holding Bones to a handful of points. Bones was so disgusted that he benched himself in the fourth quarter. In the second game, later in the season, Coach didn't call for the press. I think he knew that, even with Bones scoring, we could still win. Bones scored twenty-eight points. We won. We were a scoring machine! We were a good team, but were we a championship team?

We found out when we traveled to play Park Falls in their

cracker box gym. Park Falls won the game. I was disgusted. We had scored over fifty points and lost the game! For me, this game showed the chink in our armor.

For Coach, the game and the season must have been pure frustration. He had a starting five all with athletic talent and experience. Coach, whose hallmark was defense, was not successful in getting this terrific scoring machine team to play strong defense. When the scoring machine was on, we won; when it was off, we lost.

The news reporters who looked at win - loss statistics, ranked this Ashland team fifth in the state. The game, pitting fifth ranking Ashland against fourth ranking Superior Central, was the game of the year in northern Wisconsin. The Oredockers, undefeated in Dodd Gym, easily continued their winning streak. It looked like we were jelling.

During the warm-up of the next game, our first game with Ironwood, at Ironwood, Coach took me by the elbow and said, "Stu, you take Henderson, number 14, and pick him up as he crosses the center line." He went on to say, "Get right on top of him and don't let him shoot a set shot."

I asked, "What if he drives by me?"

He responded, "If he even tries to drive, you take a time out and I'll tell you what to do!"

This assignment left me puzzled, but I had long ago learned to follow his instructions. When the game began I picked up Henderson as instructed and, to my amazement, he didn't try to drive by me even after he learned that he couldn't get a shot. Henderson finished the game with one shot and no points. We won easily.

When we got home I asked Dad how he knew Henderson wouldn't drive past me. I knew he had never seen Henderson play. He explained that he had been watching the box scores of the Ironwood games and noticed that Henderson scored four, five or more field goals per game and seldom had a free throw. From that simple fact, he reasoned that Henderson didn't drive often and we could pick him up and guard him tight. This was clear to a former blind man; to those of us who could always see, including Coach's peers, it wasn't!

In the last game of the regular season we played away at Rhinelander. We hadn't seen Rhinelander play and had no idea what type of team they were or how they played. It didn't make any difference. Our scoring machine was in high gear. Everything we threw in the air went in the basket. We won by about twenty points.

We were ready for the regional tournament at Superior Central. Central was favored to win by virtue of having home court advantage, but we had beaten Hurley and Superior East twice and Central once so some considered us co-favorites. Central opened with East and won easily. We played Hurley in the other opening game. We were a heavy favorite, but I was leery. Hurley had started the season very inexperienced. We had beaten them twice this season, but by now they had gained experience and they were strong on defense. Coach knew you couldn't take Hurley lightly, especially with the distraction of the game against Superior Central looming the next night.

Sure enough, Hurley's strategy threw us off. They outfoxed us by switching Florian Helinski from guard to center and switching their normal center to forward. This weakened our already average defense. Their strategy worked! Our two leading scorers, John McDermott and Larry Lindholm, fouled out in the third quarter. We had a good lead going into the fourth quarter, but all of a sudden we were the smaller, less experienced team and we had lost our two top scorers. In a hard fought quarter, Hurley finally gained the lead in the last thirty seconds. The scoreboard showed a three point Hurley victory. They had simply out thought us. Just that fast our season was over!

Central easily beat Hurley and won the regional tournament. Surprisingly, they lost to Rhinelander in the sectional, a team we had beaten on their home court three weeks earlier by twenty points.

NEITHER HURLEY NOR ASHLAND WOULD BE IN THE STATE TOURNAMENT FINALS, but another small North Woods team, St. Croix Falls, won the championship. In the twelve years since the beginning of the statewide tournament, four North Woods teams had won this tournament: Rhinelander in 1939, Reedsville in 1946, Hurley in 1949 and St. Croix Falls in 1950. In the seven Wisconsin State Basketball finals from 1943 through 1949, Hurley and Ashland high schools participated six times, placing first once, second once, third twice and fourth twice. What an incredible accomplishment, considering that neither Hurley nor Ashland had ever participated in the finals prior to 1943 and were never to return to the finals after 1949!

Friday, March 5, 1965

Last Remains of Montreal Mine

About the only thing left to remind local people of ~~the Montreal Mine are waste piles similar to stock piles~~, shown above. The above photo was taken in the "good old days?" when ore was being loaded to ship out.

By 1964 the only thing left to remind local people of the mines were the "ghostly" slag piles.

CHAPTER 12

END OF AN ERA
1950-1951

TIMES WERE CHANGING in Wisconsin high school athletics. The high school consolidation movement which began in the early 1940s eliminated many small schools. Diminishing finances closed many private schools. All this resulted in fewer, but larger high schools. Rule changes in football and basketball tended to favor larger schools, making it much more difficult for the smaller high schools to compete. Conditions similar to the 1940s no longer existed in Wisconsin high school athletics. Finally, the WIAA introduced the class system for all athletic contests in Wisconsin high schools. The great David and Goliath match ups of the 1940s were a thing of the past!

In the fall of 1951 Dad took the head football coaching job at Superior State Teacher's College. His days at Hurley and Ashland high schools were over. Harry Conley and Bill Knoblauch were retired. Jack Kraemer and John MacDonald would soon retire and Carl Vergamini would leave Hurley High School. An era had ended!

In a few short years, the great underground mines of the Gogebic Range closed. The big ore docks at Ashland started coming down. The great trees were gone, the young people left, cities shrunk to shadows of their previous populations. The area stagnated. A once vibrant area was, regrettably, dying.

The North Woods would regenerate itself. By 2000 the big trees were remerging and wild life, long gone, was returning. Eventually new mines will open. More importantly, new generations of people will return and a new chapter in the North Woods will begin.

Maggie, Stu and Tom displaying the
Wisconsin Coach's Football Hall of Fame
plaque in honor of their Dad, 1981

CHAPTER 13

WHEN ALL IS SAID AND DONE

WHAT WAS IT THAT MADE ROY MELVIN such a unique coach? Many others had coached at small schools and coached multiple sports. Some had better win - loss records or won more championships. All good coaches stressed discipline, conditioning, team-play and sportsmanship. Fundamentals and techniques were taught. Even scouting was quite common. So what was it?

It was his thinking and concepts. He adapted his system to the players, not the players to his system. Few coaches, then or now, have this approach. It was Dad's innovation that permitted this unusual approach. His innovations assisted him in getting more or all players actively involved in the game. In both offense and defense most, or all, of his football and basketball players were actively involved in the play.

In football and basketball the team with the ball (offense)

almost always had the initiative, forcing the defense to react. Dad's concepts reversed this. Whenever he had reasonably comparable talent, his team had the initiative in both offense and defense.

In the final analysis Dad figured out that the essence of successful football and basketball was control of the ball. That was his overall goal. All of his innovations and strategies worked toward this goal: controlling the ball regardless of who possessed it. What a concept!

As a consummate teacher, he gave simple instructions to the individual players. His players were seldom confused or hesitant in executing his concepts. The complexity and confusion were the opponents' problems.

THE LASTING LEGACY OF SMALL TOWN HIGH SCHOOL COACHES went far beyond the game. For many, and certainly for Roy Melvin, athletics helped young men prepare for life and education was the bedrock of that preparation.

Of the thousand or more boys who played for Dad at Hurley and Ashland, all but those who entered early military service in World War II, graduated from high school, many with honors. Many went on to college and a high percentage graduated, some with advanced degrees. Charlie Yderstad reminisced that "only one of our group of twelve seniors did not go on to college." Dad not only encouraged players to go to college, but frequently helped them get scholarships, jobs or financial assistance to make college possible.

Dad embraced the Hurley High School motto: "The purpose of our high school is to train pupils to do better what they will be called upon to do in later life." Education was highly valued, especially by immigrant Americans. It's what the community wanted, what the parents wanted, what the teachers wanted, what the children got.

BY THE MID-1930S IN HURLEY AND THE MID-1940S IN ASHLAND, Dad had established full athletic programs which included football in the fall, basketball in the winter, track and tennis in the spring, and American Legion baseball and city recreation programs in the summer. If Dad found a boy with a particular talent or interest, he tried to develop that talent. In most small schools there were no swim teams, but Dad once had a swimmer who became a state champion – probably the only swimmer to do so without the benefit of a pool for training.

All across America coaches taught during the school day and coached after school hours. Why did men like John McDonald at Park Falls, Harry Conley at Superior Central, Jack Kraemer at Ironwood and the many tens of thousands of others spend the main part of their working careers coaching high school athletics? It certainly wasn't money! Dad's maximum extra pay for all sports was $700 per year, less than $1.00 per hour. It wasn't glory. Most toiled in obscurity their entire careers. Was it ego? Possibly! Whatever the reasons, their players, schools and communities were the beneficiaries. They had an impact. They made a difference.

Almost forty years after he had played for Dad, George Papadakis wrote: "I have many treasured memories of Coach and hardly a week goes by that I don't use one of his 'Melvinisms' or a technique of his. I owe 'Mel' a debt of gratitude for whatever I have achieved in life. He made me feel like a 'winner' and I love him dearly for that!"

Dad strongly believed that the game belonged to the players and that sports should be fun. All he asked of the players was to play fair and as hard as they could. Winning would take care of itself. He taught that winners should be gracious and, if they had played hard, losers could hold their heads up high. He expected more from the talented players. He used encouragement as a primary motivator and didn't chastise players. Trust was at the heart of Dad's approach. He once said, "In Hurley I could tell the players to eat grass and they would do it...and then ask why."

His influence went beyond his players. On one occasion the local doctor came to our house and asked him if he would talk to the parents of a young girl who had a nasty compound fracture of her arm. The family's religious beliefs wouldn't permit the doctor to set the girl's arm. Without medical intervention the doctor knew the girl would be crippled for life. Dad visited the family and discussed the situation with the parents. After listening to their point of view, Dad said, "If God had wanted the girl to have a crippled arm, she would have been born with it." This convinced the parents to let the doctor set their daughter's arm.

Dad was very effective at teaching life's lessons. He was a master at picking the most effective time to teach a lesson. I was on the receiving end of many more lessons in life than in sports. Sometimes his lessons caught on immediately and others took time. I was forty-three years old when his last lesson got through to me. I can still hear myself saying "that's what he meant" when the light went on!

Over the years Dad received many letters from his colleagues and players. The letters frequently reflect on lessons learned from Coach. It is clear that is what people remember most about Dad.

Dad enjoyed an excellent reputation with his peers. Prior to Dad's induction into the Wisconsin Football Coaches Hall of Fame, Harold F. Connors wrote:

> Roy Melvin came to Hurley as a Coach of the high school athletics in the fall of 1923. I was principal of Hurley High school all of the time that "Coach" Melvin worked in Hurley. Leaving Hurley he coached athletics in Ashland and later went on to Beloit. Coach was a gentleman. He set a splendid example of personal behavior for his students to emulate. He had an abiding faith in the integrity of modern youth and loved to work with teenage boys and girls. He hammered home the importance of good sportsmanship. He insisted that his teams be scrupulously fair and honest in their mutual relationships and with their competitors. I can't recall that he ever had a major disciplinary problem in Hurley.
>
> In our city everybody likes Roy Melvin. He built a great tradition of fine clean athletics. In my judgment he is eminently worthy of a place in the Wisconsin Coach's Hall of Fame.

Probably the most significant measure of Dad is the regard in which he is held by his former players and students.

John H. Gustafson remembers:

> Most young fellows getting direction, instruction, and guidance from a man like Roy Melvin, cannot possibly know when they will test or try or put that valuable counsel to work for themselves. Mine came when I began to coach my own teams. I found out that Roy Melvin knew more about preparing young men for the game at that moment and for the game of life that was to follow, than any of the various coaches I had after him.
>
> He was way ahead of his time, in so many ways, with his innovations in practice and in games. As I see it now—his insights and imagination and his ability to demonstrate what he wanted done were the keys to his success. The man was miles ahead of his fellow coaches. He spent hours telling me

why a ball had to be held a certain way, kicked a certain way or hit a certain way to achieve maximum efficiency. Even if it had been a bowling ball or a cue ball he would have known how far the skid and how many turns for the best efficiency.

But above all, that combination of ingredients that goes to keep teams in winning circles, Roy was a man of honor and wit – a real true friend to all of us. I'll never forget those cracked brown shoes and that special rabbit's foot—ever.

My deepest regret is that I did not take the time or make the effort to write or talk to him while he was still alive, and tell him how I felt about him and how he influenced my life.

Paul Tomlinson writes:

I played for Roy in my junior and senior years at Ashland High School. I had the highest respect for Roy and felt that he could have coached at any school in the country. Roy came to Ashland from Hurley in 1942. He took over football and basketball teams with losing records and completely changed the win lose columns with practically the same players. He was always figuring out ways to score points against the opponents. He could take a mediocre team and coach them to take advantage of the other teams' weaknesses to score points that no one thought could be done. When asked, after a football victory why his team didn't make more first downs, he replied that when they start giving points for making first downs, we'll make more first downs. I don't think there is one person alive who ever played for Roy Melvin who does not think that Roy was a superb coach and a sincere friend.

Dominic Moselle in a letter to my brother Tom in 1974 shares:

I am glad to hear about your Dad because to me he still is Coach. And Tom, in the course of years of

> play I still say to everyone he was my best coach. He taught me many things and I owe all my athletic success to his teaching. Your Dad was like a father to me and I often think of those good old days. Around this area he is still remembered and his name often comes up about his great coaching ability and his ability to handle athletes.

Bruce Fossum reminisces:

> As a Coach, out of total respect I would call him nothing else, he was unparalleled in imagination and inventiveness along with the unfathomable skill of being able to teach young men. He was ages ahead of his time. He knew how to put points on the board with new inventive methods and yet he really was successful because he knew how to put fundamentals first. When I got into the same business I used to call him frequently and visit him as often as I could to receive yet another coaching clinic. In our last get together in Beloit about two months before he died he again reminded me always keep my chin up and stand up for what I believed — a lesson often repeated throughout my formative years. My two sons met him on that trip and I only wish that their lives could have been touched a bit more by this man, just as he so indelibly touched mine. I watched him develop men rather than use them. He was a second Dad, a demanding task master when necessary, a loyal friend. Yes, the most revered man in my life. He did not forget his players. They were his sons.

Dad had his share of wins and losses, but the measure of his success was summed up by John Chapple, editor and publisher of the *Ashland Daily Press*:

> Roy Melvin had the finest influence on young people in Ashland of any man I have ever known. He taught them to be clean and honest and good sportsmen

> and good losers when losses occurred. He lifted the level not only of those he coached but the whole student body. His occasional talks to students on what makes a worthwhile life were masterpieces of encouragement and uplift. I am sure that he saved many young people from negative influences and disastrous misdirection. Roy Melvin was one of the great men in Ashland's history.

Dad was not only a coach for all seasons, he was a coach for all students!

EPILOGUE

WHEN THE WISCONSIN HIGH SCHOOL COACHES ASSOCIATION awarded Roy Melvin their Certificate of Merit, President Marlon Batterman ended the award presentation with this sentence: "The complete extent of his contributions to coaching will never be known or fully appreciated, but he will always serve as a symbol of what is desirable and honorable in the coaching profession." It couldn't have been said better!

Although his technical coaching achievements were considerable, it was his impact on his players, school, and the community that was truly remarkable.

Dad died quietly in January, 1975 at the age of 78. Six years later, he was inducted into the Wisconsin Football Coaches Hall of Fame, a fitting tribute to a man whose life was devoted to high school athletics. As his friend and fellow coach, Walter "Wadz" Martens, said at the second annual induction ceremony, "He should have been a charter member, but we corrected that this year."

Although he was held in the highest regard by his peers, it was his players who paid the highest tribute to his success as a coach. During the spring and summer of 1946 millions of men returned home from World War II. Many of Dad's former players visited our home in Ashland to see him, and in many cases, ask his advice. One particular visit stands out in my mind. A former U. S. Army Air Corps pilot had just left the house after presenting Dad with all his service medals, saying, "Here Coach, you earned these!" These medals included, among many, the Distinguished Flying Cross and a Purple Heart.

With tears in his eyes, Dad said to me, "This makes it all worthwhile." He then showed me the contents of the velvet lined walnut box with all the medals.

I asked him, "What are you going to do with them?"

He answered, "I'll wait a few weeks and then drive to Hurley and give the medals to his parents."

I believe that was his finest moment!

Many years later a former player and classmate of mine said to me, "You know, Stu, you're lucky."

I asked him, "Lucky about what?"

He said, "We had Coach a few hours a day for a few years, but you had him twenty- four hours a day, forever."

I was lucky. Coach was also a great Dad!

The author, Stuart Melvin, is the oldest son of Coach Roy Melvin and played athletics for his Dad four years in the late 1940s. He continues to pursue his enthusiasm for all sports, and has a keen interest in history and the outdoors. He lives in Denver with his Scottish born wife, Eleanor, and spends his summers in the seaside town of Largs, Scotland, This book was prompted by his younger sister, Maggie, who was fascinated by tales of her Dad's coaching.

ISBN 142511102-5
9 781425 111021